# Contents

# Simply The Best

*Remembering Tina Turner — The 83 Moments Of My Life*

Maya Morgan

# Copyright

**Simply The Best:** Remembering Tina Turner – The 83 Pivotal Moments in my Life and Career

# Introduction

It is with a profound sense of loss, yet an enduring spirit of admiration, that we pen these words. On May 24, 2023, the world bid farewell to an exceptional soul, a dazzling star in the constellation of music – Tina Turner.

Born with a voice that thundered and soared, and a spirit that danced with resilience and strength, Tina was more than a gifted artist. She was a beacon of perseverance, an embodiment of grace, and a testament to the human capacity to triumph over adversity.

This book is a tribute to her indomitable spirit, an attempt to echo the power of her legacy, and a celebration of her unforgettable journey. From humble beginnings to the pinnacle of stardom, Tina Turner's story is an inspirational symphony that continues to resonate, echoing her message of courage and resilience.

Though we mourn her passing, this is not a book of grief. Instead, it is a homage to a life lived to the fullest, a testament to an unwavering spirit that scaled the heights of success, and a tribute to a heart that sang the most harmonious tunes. As we turn these pages, we remember Tina Turner, the woman who was, truly, 'Simply the Best.'

# PART 01: Early Life Of Tina Turner

# Moment Nr. 1

## The Birth of a Star on November 26, 1939

There is a certain magic in the hills of Tennessee that has gifted the world with legendary artists, and on November 26, 1939, in the small town of Nutbush, the tiny sparks of this magic came together to create one of the brightest stars to ever grace the music world. This was the day that Anna Mae Bullock, who the world would come to know as Tina Turner, was born.

Her birth, during the twilight years of the Great Depression, bore witness to the resilience that would be her life's theme. She was born into an era and place where adversity was commonplace, a world that would shape her spirit, mould her character, and ultimately, fuel her rise to stardom.

In a tiny shotgun house, built by her father, she first drew breath. This modest beginning was a far cry from the glittering stages and packed arenas she would one day conquer. And yet, in this humble setting, a radiant force was born, one that would shine brilliantly and touch millions.

From her earliest days, Tina displayed an unquenchable spirit. As a child, she sang in the church choir, her voice echoing through the wooden rafters, a prelude to the powerful, raw vocals that would later define her career. Her voice was pure and untamed, and it filled the modest church with a fervor that hinted at the passion and power she would bring to her performances in the years to come.

Growing up in Nutbush offered few opportunities, but Tina, ever the dreamer, saw beyond the cotton fields and gravel roads. She had a vision, fueled by the music she heard on the radio, and carried by the rhythm that seemed to pulsate in her veins. She knew, even then, that she was meant for something greater. Her talent was undeniable, her resolve unshakeable.

The story of Tina Turner is one of transformation and triumph. Born Anna Mae Bullock, she would rise from the humblest of beginnings to become an icon, a beacon of strength and determination. She would captivate audiences worldwide with her electrifying performances, defy societal norms, and become a symbol of empowerment for countless women.

November 26, 1939, marks not only the birth of a remarkable woman but also the genesis of a profound cultural shift. With every step Tina Turner took on her journey from Nutbush to global fame, she transformed the world around her, and in doing so, became one of the most influential women in music history.

Her life serves as an enduring testament to the human spirit's resilience. This was the dawn of a life that would inspire, uplift, and ultimately, reshape the musical landscape. We remember her not just as the Queen of Rock and Roll, but as an indomitable spirit who embodied the phrase 'Simply the Best' in every facet of her life. And so, we begin our tribute to Tina Turner, a woman whose life was a melody of strength, grace, and unparalleled talent.

# Moment Nr. 2

## *Brown Sugar and Sweet Rhode Island Red: Tina's Childhood Nicknames and Their Influence on Her Developing Persona*

In the humble beginnings of Nutbush, Tennessee, Tina Turner, known then as Anna Mae Bullock, began to shape her persona, encouraged by a blend of southern traditions, spirited community, and a natural sense of performance. Throughout her childhood, Tina was affectionately known by two nicknames: "Brown Sugar" and "Sweet Rhode Island Red." These endearing monikers not only added flavor to her childhood but also became significant cornerstones in the formation of her vibrant personality and resilient spirit.

"Brown Sugar," a name fondly given to her due to her complexion and sweet nature, held within it the essence of Tina's unique identity. This nickname was symbolic of the rich cultural heritage that she carried with pride. It was indicative of her roots and the wholesome, earthy charm that was as intrinsic to Tina as the music she loved. It also held a sense of sweetness that was echoed in her disposition, a trait that was as enticing as her voice and would endear her to millions around the world.

"Sweet Rhode Island Red," the other moniker, was an embodiment of Tina's fiery spirit and her boundless energy. It spoke of her vibrant personality, the captivating charisma she brought to every performance, and her commanding presence that was impossible to ignore. Just like the Rhode Island Red hen, known for its hardiness and spirit, Tina was a dynamo, a bundle of raw, untamed energy. This nickname was a testament to her determination, resilience, and the flame of passion that burned within her.

Tina's nicknames were not mere labels. They were a blueprint of her soul, a harbinger of the persona she would grow into, and the indomitable spirit that would form the cornerstone of her extraordinary journey. They were the seeds that would germinate into the legendary Tina Turner, an artist whose persona was just as captivating as her music.

Tina Turner's life was a symphony of powerful performances, boundless energy, and a spirit that refused to be anything less than 'Simply The Best.' From her humble beginnings in Nutbush, through every trial, triumph, and transformation, she remained a beacon of strength, resilience, and empowerment. Her nicknames, 'Brown Sugar' and 'Sweet Rhode Island Red,' were an embodiment of her essence, a testament to her spirit, and a glimpse into the life of a girl who would become a global music sensation.

Tina's story is one of unwavering courage, unyielding determination, and an unwavering faith in herself. It's a story that began in a small town but reached the farthest corners of the globe, touching millions of hearts along the way. In every note, in every performance, and in every moment of her remarkable life, Tina Turner was, and always will be, 'Simply the Best.'

# Moment Nr. 3

## *The Strength of Her Mother: The Impact of Zelma Bullock on Young Tina*

In the narrative of Tina Turner's life, one character stands out not just as a parent but as a beacon of fortitude and resilience. This is Zelma Bullock, Tina's mother, a figure whose strength was as enduring as the Tennessee hills they called home.

From the start, Zelma had an unyielding will and an unbreakable spirit. She was a woman hardened by circumstances yet tempered with a unique blend of compassion and determination. These traits not only defined Zelma Bullock but also left an indelible imprint on young Tina.

Tina's early years were far from easy, shaped by hardship and marred by adversity. Yet, amidst this challenging backdrop, Zelma's resilience provided a source of inspiration and solace. Zelma's stead-fastness in the face of adversity, her undying spirit in the throes of hardship, taught Tina an invaluable lesson: that strength was not just about physical prowess but also about the power of the heart and the resolve of the spirit.

The strength of Zelma Bullock was a quiet yet potent force. It was found in the stern, encouraging words she spoke, the tireless work she did, and the silent sacrifices she made. It was in these quiet acts of courage that Tina found the blueprint for her own brand of strength, a strength that would become her armor in the years to come.

Zelma's influence extended beyond mere survival. She instilled in Tina a love for music, the gift that would become the young star's escape and ultimate vehicle for self-expression. Under her mother's watchful eye, Tina began to sing in their church's choir, her voice carrying the weight of their shared experiences, yet resonating with an undeniable hope. This was the first spark of Tina's incredible musical journey, ignited and fanned by Zelma's guidance.

Tina Turner, the Queen of Rock 'n' Roll, the woman who would mesmerize audiences worldwide, was born of Zelma Bullock's strength. Zelma's indomitable spirit, mirrored in Tina's own resilience, became an integral part of the music sensation's persona.


Tina Turner's life was a powerful symphony of resilience and transformation. Her story echoes her mother's strength and embodies the endurance and determination that was passed down to her. As we delve into the life of this remarkable woman, we celebrate not only Tina Turner, but also the strength of the woman who raised her, the woman who helped shape a music legend. Tina's journey from Nutbush to global stardom is a testament to the power of inherited strength, a tribute to her mother, and proof that even in the toughest of soils, beautiful and strong flowers can bloom.

# Moment Nr. 4

---

## *The Absence of Her Father: The Departure of Richard Bullock and Its Effects on Her*

In the heart-wrenching narrative of Tina Turner's early life, the absence of her father, Richard Bullock, was a crucial element that shaped her journey. Richard's departure, a pivotal event in Tina's life, was a catalyst that brought both pain and a profound sense of determination that would later become a driving force in her life.

Richard Bullock was a hard-working man, whose work often took him away from home, resulting in periods of his absence during Tina's early life. However, it was his ultimate departure that left a void, a feeling of absence that the young Anna Mae would carry with her. This departure wasn't merely physical; it was a void of paternal guidance and warmth, a lack that left indelible marks on Tina's spirit.

Growing up in a father-absent home was a challenge, a series of trials that tested and molded Tina's resilience. This absence, though heartrending, began to shape a core of steel within her, an unyielding determination that would later manifest itself in her journey towards stardom.

Tina's formative years were spent under the shadows of her father's absence, but it was here that her resilience began to take root. The trials she encountered, the struggles she braved, instilled in her a tenacity and a willpower that were nothing short of extraordinary. The absence of her father became a wellspring from which she drew strength and determination.

Amidst the pain of her father's absence, Tina found music as her refuge. The soulful tunes and stirring lyrics were her solace, a way to fill the silence that her father's absence had left. It was this absence that fueled her passion for music, turning her pain into powerful performances that would captivate audiences worldwide.

The departure of Richard Bullock from Tina Turner's life was a loss, but it was also a profound catalyst for growth. It was the seed of adversity from which sprung the extraordinary resilience and determination that would define Tina's life. Her story isn't just one of loss and absence, but of triumph over adversity, of transforming pain into power.

Tina Turner, the unstoppable force, the Queen of Rock 'n' Roll, was born from the ashes of loss and the seeds of resilience. Her father's absence was a significant chapter in her story, but it was her response to this loss, her transformation of absence into strength, that truly defined her journey. Tina Turner's early life may have been marked by her father's departure, but it was her resilience, her unyielding spirit that emerged from this loss, which made her 'Simply the Best'.

# Moment Nr. 5

## *A Life in Nutbush: Exploring the Influence of Her Tennessee Upbringing*

Tina Turner was born Anna Mae Bullock in a quaint, bucolic town called Nutbush, located in the heartland of Tennessee. While the world knows her as the indomitable Queen of Rock 'n' Roll, her early life in Nutbush was instrumental in shaping the remarkable woman she would become.

Nutbush was not just a town; it was the backdrop of Tina's formative years. It was here, amidst cotton fields and the soulful hymns of her local church choir, that young Anna Mae first found her voice. The landscape of Nutbush, with its vast fields and deep southern culture, nurtured her spirit, imparting values of hard work, resilience, and unyielding determination.

Her humble beginnings in Nutbush were far from the glitz and glamour that would later become synonymous with Tina Turner. Here, life was marked by the rhythm of the seasons and the toil of hard work. These formative years, while tough, ingrained in her an uncompromising work ethic and an unwavering sense of grit that would propel her to stardom.

However, Nutbush offered more than lessons of resilience and hard work. It was in the choir of her local Baptist church that Tina first fell in love with music. The stirring gospel hymns, the spirit of communal celebration, and the emotional richness of these experiences ignited in her a passion for music. They gave a young, dream-filled Tina an outlet for her emotions, a space where she could truly express herself.

And express herself she did. Even as a child, Tina's voice was powerfully unique, filled with a raw and palpable emotion that moved anyone who heard it. Nutbush, with its roots deep in the tradition of gospel music, nurtured this talent, setting the stage for the magnificent performer she would become.

The narrative of Tina Turner's life cannot be told without acknowledging the powerful influence of her Tennessee upbringing. Nutbush was where the roots of her strength were formed, where her love for music was nurtured, and where the seeds of her dreams were first sown. It was in this small Tennessee town that Tina Turner, the global music sensation, took her first steps towards becoming 'Simply the Best.'

Tina's journey from Nutbush to the world stage is a testament to her indomitable spirit, a spirit born and bred in the heartland of Tennessee. Her story is not just about the rise of a music legend; it is also the story of a small-town girl who dared to dream beyond the cotton fields of Nutbush and, with her incredible talent and unwavering resolve, turned those dreams into reality.

The essence of Nutbush, its lessons of resilience, and its rich musical heritage lived on in Tina, reflecting in her music and her extraordinary life. This small town, with its immense impact, lives on in every song she sang, in every stage she commanded, and in every heart, she touched with her music.

# Moment Nr. 6

## *The Discovery of Her Voice: Her First Solo in the Church Choir*

The music world remembers Tina Turner as a roaring volcano of talent, but this volcano was once a spark, a spark that ignited during a humble church choir performance in Nutbush, Tennessee. Even at an early age, Tina Turner, then known as Anna Mae Bullock, possessed a voice that hinted at the power and passion she would later bring to the world stage.

Inside the Spring Hill Baptist Church, where the community congregated every Sunday, young Anna Mae discovered a sanctuary where her voice could soar freely. In the gospel hymns, she found her emotional outlet, a refuge from her challenging early life. The church was her first audience, and the choir was her first band, the fertile ground where the seed of her talent took root and started to grow.

The day of her first solo was a turning point. Standing before the congregation, Anna Mae felt a mix of fear and excitement. She was a bundle of nerves, yet she held within her a fire, a potent force that was waiting to be unleashed. And when she opened her mouth to sing, that fire blazed forth in a voice so powerful it echoed off the church walls, leaving the congregation stunned.

The melody was steeped in the traditions of gospel, but the voice...the voice was uniquely her own. It was deep, raw, and full of emotion that belied her young age. It was a voice that could make the heart ache, the soul stir, and the spirit rise. That day, the congregation didn't just hear Anna Mae; they felt her, touched by the profound depth of emotion she poured into her performance.

The echoes of her voice in the church heralded the birth of a star. Anna Mae Bullock, the little girl from Nutbush, had found her calling. She had discovered the power of her voice, and from that moment, she knew that singing wasn't just something she did; it was who she was.

This early solo performance was not just about showcasing her talent; it was a revelation, a glimpse into the depth of her soul. It marked the beginning of Tina Turner's journey, a journey that would see her rise from the cotton fields of Nutbush to the pinnacle of global stardom.

Remembering this pivotal moment in her life, we understand that Tina Turner was not merely a performer; she was an embodiment of the power of music, the transformative ability of a voice steeped in passion and resilience. From her first solo in the church choir to her last stunning performance, Tina's voice was a beacon of strength, inspiring millions around the world.

In Nutbush, in that small Baptist church, Tina Turner took her first step towards her extraordinary destiny. The girl with the powerful voice evolved into the woman with the indomitable spirit, who would forever leave her mark on the world of music.

And so, we celebrate not just the incredible performer Tina became, but also Anna Mae, the young choirgirl from Nutbush, whose passion and strength began stirring within her long before the world came to know her as Tina Turner, the Queen of Rock 'n' Roll.

# PART 02: The Beginnings of Tina's Career

# Moment Nr. 7

## *The Night She Met Ike: The Chance Meeting That Changed Her Destiny*

In the story of Tina Turner, one night stands out as a significant crossroads. This was the night she met Ike Turner, a charismatic musician whose band, the Kings of Rhythm, was making waves in St. Louis, Missouri. Ike Turner was a force of nature, an indomitable presence on stage, and his path crossing with Tina's would have profound implications on both their lives.

In the summer of 1957, Anna Mae Bullock and her sister Alline attended a show at the Manhattan Club in East St. Louis. The atmosphere was electric. The Kings of Rhythm were on stage, their infectious rhythm and blues setting the room alight. The club was buzzing with energy, but no one knew that destiny was at work, and a star was about to be born.

The pivotal moment came when Ike invited audience members to sing with his band. It was a common practice to keep the crowd entertained, but on this night, it would change the course of music history. Encouraged by Alline, Anna Mae seized the opportunity. Ike was hesitant at first - he hadn't heard her sing before. But what came next took his breath away.

Anna Mae stepped up and delivered a performance that was nothing short of astonishing. She sang with a raw passion and soulful intensity that left the room spellbound. Her voice, powerful and vibrant, commanded attention and resonated with Ike. He was so impressed that he immediately asked her to join the band. That night, Anna Mae Bullock stepped off the stage not just as a singer but as a burgeoning star.

The meeting with Ike Turner was a turning point. From this chance encounter sprang the Ike & Tina Turner Revue, an act that would go on to dazzle audiences with its electrifying performances and shape the soundscape of rock and soul music.

Yet, this meeting was not only about Tina's career taking flight. It was also the start of a complex and turbulent relationship with Ike. Their partnership would push Tina to her limits, testing her strength and resilience in ways she could never have imagined. But as we would come to see, it would ultimately set the stage for her triumphant solo career.

The night she met Ike, Tina Turner stood on the precipice of an extraordinary journey. It was a journey fraught with challenges, but one that she navigated with extraordinary grace and determination. It was a journey that saw her transform from Anna Mae Bullock, a young singer from Nutbush, Tennessee, into Tina Turner, an icon whose music and spirit would touch the lives of millions.

As we look back on that night, we celebrate Tina's courage, her resilience, and her indomitable spirit. We honor her journey, recognizing that every twist and turn, every high and low, contributed to the remarkable woman she became. In her story, we find inspiration, a testament to the power of resilience and the enduring spirit of human potential.

# Moment Nr. 8

## *Becoming Tina: The Story Behind Her Transformative Name Change*

A name holds power. It becomes an identity, a personal brand. When young Anna Mae Bullock adopted the stage name "Tina Turner," she was unknowingly choosing a name that would resonate around the world, a name that would become synonymous with resilience, talent, and fiery energy.

Anna Mae Bullock became Tina Turner in 1960, but the decision was not entirely hers. The one who envisioned the name was none other than Ike Turner. He had been swept away by Anna's riveting performance at the Manhattan Club and sought to shape her into a star he believed she could be.

The name "Tina" was inspired by the television character Sheena, Queen of the Jungle - a symbol of strength, independence, and allure. These were traits Ike saw in Anna. The surname "Turner," Ike's own, was added as a symbol of their professional partnership. It was a pragmatic move on Ike's part. The name would provide continuity for the act even if the singer changed - a fact Tina later discovered was written into their contract.

While the name was conceived strategically, it soon took on a life of its own. As Tina, Anna Mae started to carve a niche in the world of music. The name seemed to galvanize her spirit, her audacity on stage perfectly embodied in this alter ego. With this newly crafted identity, Tina began to transcend her humble beginnings. She was no longer the shy girl from Nutbush, Tennessee. On stage, she was Tina Turner, the dynamic, indomitable performer who captivated audiences with her electrifying presence.

However, this transformation was not without its struggles. As Tina's star rose, the tumultuous relationship with Ike became increasingly complex. The same name that bound them in a dynamic professional partnership also became a symbol of the control and abuse Tina suffered behind closed doors. Despite the turmoil, Tina held on to her stage name, even after her turbulent marriage to Ike ended.

In her own words, she had "fought hard" for the name. It was more than a stage name; it was a symbol of her journey, her struggles, and her triumphs. To Tina, it represented the woman she had become — a woman who rose above adversity to build a legendary career.

And so, Tina Turner she remained. The girl born as Anna Mae Bullock may have been assigned her famous name, but it was her indomitable spirit, relentless resilience, and transformative talent that truly defined it. Tina Turner, the name, became a legacy of strength and survival, inspiring millions worldwide. Every time the name "Tina Turner" echoed on stage, it celebrated the woman who had journeyed far from her hometown to the pinnacle of the music world, always staying simply the best.

# Moment Nr. 9

## *A Fool in Love: The Breakout Hit that Launched Ike & Tina Turner*

One can't tell the story of Tina Turner without a mention of "A Fool in Love," the electrifying breakout hit that marked the beginning of her meteoric rise to stardom. Released in 1960, the song was a stepping stone for the Ike & Tina Turner Revue, a launchpad that sent them hurtling towards the stratosphere of musical fame.

The story behind "A Fool in Love" is as captivating as the song itself. It was initially meant to feature Ike Turner's regular vocalist, Art Lassiter. When Lassiter didn't show up to the recording session, a young and enthusiastic Tina, then known as Anna Mae, stepped in to sing the song as a guide track. Her intention was merely to lay down a blueprint for the official singer. What she didn't realize was that she was carving her path towards an illustrious music career.

Tina's raw and powerful rendition of "A Fool in Love" was nothing short of captivating. Her passionate delivery, filled with emotional depth and incredible vocal range, left everyone in the studio in awe, including Ike Turner and the producer, Juggy Murray. Realizing they had stumbled upon a gold mine of talent, the decision was made to release the song as it was, with Tina's fiery vocals in the forefront.

"A Fool in Love" was a sensation. The song debuted on the Billboard Hot 100 chart and quickly climbed its way up to the number two spot on the R&B chart. It marked the arrival of Ike & Tina Turner as a formidable force in the music industry, setting the tone for the iconic duo's future successes.

Beyond its commercial success, "A Fool in Love" was significant for another reason. It was a showcase for Tina's distinctive vocal style - raw, gritty, and soulful, a clear departure from the polished, restrained style that dominated the pop charts at the time. It was a statement, a proclamation that Tina Turner was here, and she had something unique to bring to the table.

"A Fool in Love" was not just a song, it was a pivotal moment in Tina's life. It marked the beginning of her journey from a small-town girl to a global music sensation. The song was a declaration of her talent, an assertion of her fiery spirit, and a testament to her potential. It was the dawn of an era, the birth of a star.

Tina Turner's life was forever altered by that one unanticipated recording session. She stepped into the studio that day as Anna Mae Bullock, a backup singer with dreams in her eyes. She walked out as Tina Turner, the powerhouse vocalist behind a chart-topping hit, her name on the cusp of becoming a household term. Such is the power of a song, such is the power of "A Fool in Love."

# PART 03: The Ike & Tina Turner Revue

# Moment Nr. 10

## The Revue's Peak: Chart-topping Hits and Relentless Touring

The 1960s was a golden era for Tina Turner and the Ike & Tina Turner Revue. Riding high on the success of "A Fool in Love," the ensemble was on fire, churning out chart-topping hits and packing concert halls with relentless touring. It was a period of seemingly unstoppable momentum, a time when Tina's blazing star shone the brightest.

The Revue's trademark blend of rhythm and blues, soul, and rock 'n' roll struck a chord with the audience. Songs like "It's Gonna Work Out Fine," "I Idolize You," and "Poor Fool" cemented their position in the music scene. These hits, interspersed with electrifying live performances, propelled the Ike & Tina Turner Revue to new heights of stardom.

Their live performances were legendary. The Revue was known for their dynamic stage presence, high-energy routines, and, above all, Tina's raw, powerful vocals. Each concert was a spectacle, showcasing not only Tina's vocal prowess but her electrifying stage presence. Dancing with fervor and singing with a fiery passion, Tina held the audience in the palm of her hand. She was a force of nature, the very epitome of the powerhouse performer.

Their unyielding dedication to their craft saw them tour relentlessly. They were constantly on the road, playing at small clubs, large concert halls, and everything in between. The demanding schedule was exhausting, but it reflected their determination and drive to succeed. It was a testament to Tina's indomitable spirit, her unwavering commitment to her art, and her desire to connect with her fans.

Despite the grueling tour schedule, Tina's charisma never waned. She performed each show as if it were her first, bringing the same energy, passion, and enthusiasm to every stage she stepped onto. Her performances were a manifestation of her fiery spirit, a testament to her belief that the audience deserved nothing less than her best.

This period was more than just a series of chart-topping hits and tours. It was a time of growth and evolution for Tina as an artist. She honed her craft, developed her unique vocal style, and built a solid foundation for the iconic career that was to follow.

While the public saw the glittering success of the Revue, few knew the turmoil brewing behind the scenes. But those stories come later. For now, let's celebrate this peak time in Tina's early career when her star was on a dizzying ascent, when she stood on the stage, belting out hit after hit, capturing hearts, and making music history. This was Tina Turner, in her element, at her best, proving to the world that she was, indeed, simply the best.

Their legacy was cemented with their induction into the Rock & Roll Hall of Fame in 1991. Yet, while their music was celebrated, Tina Turner was preparing for a transition that would take her to even greater heights.

The Revue's peak period served as a stepping stone for Tina's career, paving the way for her evolution as a solo artist. But that's a tale for another sub-chapter. For now, let us revel in the triumph of this period, when Tina, together with Ike and the band, created a musical revolution that would resonate for generations to come.

# Moment Nr. 11

## *River Deep – Mountain High: The Phil Spector-produced single*

In the illustrious landscape of popular music, few tracks have cut as deep or soared as high as "River Deep - Mountain High." The 1966 single, an audacious collaboration between the dynamic duo Ike and Tina Turner and legendary producer Phil Spector, was more than just a hit song. It was a musical revelation that ignited Tina Turner's career, offering a glimpse of the star's inherent magnificence in the making.

When Spector approached Ike and Tina Turner, they had already established themselves as the beating heart of rhythm and blues. However, "River Deep - Mountain High" was designed to be a departure from their roots. Spector's vision was a grandeur pop anthem that fused elements of soul, gospel, and rock to create what he termed a "Wall of Sound". Tina Turner, the shining star of the duo, was handpicked by Spector himself, recognizing her raw vocal power and unique style, qualities that would ignite the track with extraordinary life.

Recording this track was not a walk in the park. The process was rigorous, demanding, and fraught with tension. Spector was notorious for his perfectionism, and Turner, equally relentless, was determined to rise to the challenge. In a testament to her unwavering grit, Turner took on the song's monumental range, traversing musical peaks and valleys with a powerful grace that left everyone in the studio awe-struck.

Upon its release, the track didn't immediately resonate with audiences in the U.S., even though it was received warmly in the U.K. where it peaked at #3. However, its legacy wasn't defined by immediate chart success but by the extraordinary staying power that has seen it revered as a pop masterpiece in years to follow. It was a song that served as a catalyst for Turner's career, revealing her potential to move beyond the soulful rhythm and blues into a global pop phenomenon.

"River Deep - Mountain High" also marked the inception of Tina's journey to individual stardom. It was the first glimpse of the Tina Turner we now know and love - not just one half of a duo but a powerhouse in her own right. With this track, she demonstrated her ability to dominate a song, imprinting her personality and unparalleled vocal prowess on every note.

The significance of "River Deep - Mountain High" lies in its embodiment of Turner's indomitable spirit. The song, much like Turner herself, resonates with an undeniable potency and an infectious determination. Despite early challenges, it rose to achieve enduring acclaim - a fitting metaphor for Tina's life and career. From a humble beginning in Nutbush, Tennessee, Tina would climb the mountain high of international fame, becoming a symbol of resilience, perseverance, and immense talent.

From this moment onwards, Tina Turner would no longer be just a part of 'The Ike & Tina Turner Revue'. With "River Deep – Mountain High", Tina had found her voice, a thunderous, passionate roar that would continue to echo across the world for decades to come, influencing countless artists and inspiring millions of fans. This song was an emphatic declaration of Tina Turner's arrival into the global music scene, setting the stage for her to become "Simply the Best".

# Moment Nr. 12

## *Proud Mary: The making of this Grammy-winning cover*

Every music legend has that defining moment, a singular performance that etches their name indelibly into the annals of history. For Tina Turner, the iconic rock-n-roll powerhouse, that moment arrived in 1971 with a rollicking, soulful rendition of the song "Proud Mary".

Originally performed by Creedence Clearwater Revival, "Proud Mary" was a decent success when it debuted in 1969. However, when Ike & Tina Turner released their interpretation two years later, they didn't merely cover the song – they reinvented it, transforming this pleasant riverboat ballad into an electrifying anthem that would resonate across generations.

The genius behind their rendition lay in the unique arrangement of the song. The track begins with a slow, sultry preamble, with Tina's smoky vocals painting vivid imagery of people working on the river. But then, like a riverboat picking up steam, the tempo abruptly shifts into an explosive, high-energy revival. This fusion of smooth blues and energetic rock and roll was unprecedented, and it showcased Tina's versatility as an artist who could smoothly transition between different genres and moods.

"Proud Mary" was more than a song for Tina – it was a platform for her to fully express her extraordinary energy and talent. Her electrifying stage performances of the song became legendary, with audiences captivated by her fiery spirit, mesmerizing dance moves, and the raw power of her voice. It was during these performances that the world truly recognized Tina Turner's unparalleled capacity to command a stage.

In many ways, "Proud Mary" was a turning point in Turner's career. The track won the duo their first Grammy Award in 1972 for Best R&B Vocal Performance by a Group, cementing their place in the music industry. The Grammy was not just an affirmation of Turner's talent, but it also signaled the recognition she had long deserved.

But "Proud Mary" was more than just a milestone in Tina Turner's career; it was a reflection of her own journey. The lyrics resonated with Turner's tenacity and determination, embodying her spirit of constant perseverance, her readiness to keep rolling, much like the river in the song. Born in the small town of Nutbush, Tennessee, Tina had faced her share of hardships and challenges. But like the 'Proud Mary', she kept on turning, pushing through adversity, rolling with the punches, and navigating the currents of her life with grace, strength, and an unwavering resolve.

"Proud Mary" also foreshadowed Tina's future solo career, providing a glimpse into the indomitable spirit and relentless energy that would become her trademark as a solo artist. The song, much like Tina herself, was unstoppable, becoming a cultural phenomenon that has transcended time, repeatedly covered and continually loved by fans all over the world.

In the annals of music history, few songs carry the legacy that "Proud Mary" does. It's not just a Grammy-winning hit; it is a testament to Tina Turner's enduring talent and relentless spirit, a song that continues to echo the essence of this incredible woman. Through "Proud Mary", we remember Tina not just as a global music sensation, but as the unstoppable force of nature she truly was.

# PART 04: Struggles Behind the Scenes

# Moment Nr. 13

## *Unseen Battles: The Hidden Struggles within her Marriage to Ike*

Behind the dazzling lights and stirring performances of the Ike & Tina Turner Revue, a deeply personal drama unfolded, unbeknownst to millions of adoring fans. Tina Turner, the charismatic queen of rock 'n' roll, endured a turbulent, abusive marriage to Ike Turner that would test her strength, resilience, and spirit in unimaginable ways.

Born Anna Mae Bullock in the humble town of Nutbush, Tennessee, Tina was introduced to Ike Turner in St. Louis, an encounter that would dramatically alter her life's course. The duo's professional collaboration quickly bloomed into a personal relationship. But as their fame escalated, so did the severity of Ike's abusive behavior, cloaked by the glitz and glamour of their onstage personas.

Ike's control over Tina extended far beyond the stage. He sought to dictate every facet of her life, gradually eroding her autonomy and self-confidence. He renamed her 'Tina', a brand he claimed he owned. These controlling tendencies weren't merely signs of Ike's possessiveness but a reflection of the systematic abuse she endured for nearly 16 years.

Yet, in the face of such adversity, Tina demonstrated an extraordinary resilience. Amid the turmoil, she found solace in her music, channeling her pain and suffering into soul-stirring performances that captivated audiences. Her indomitable spirit was not only visible on stage but also in the relentless pursuit of her freedom.

Eventually, the struggle became unbearable, and in July 1976, Tina made a daring escape after a particularly violent altercation. She stepped into the unknown, armed only with her stage name and a resolve to rebuild her life, free from the shackles of Ike's abuse. Despite the immense challenges that lay ahead, Tina chose the path of courage, preferring uncertainty and struggle over an abusive, unfulfilling marriage.

Tina's experience with domestic violence, while heart-wrenching, is an important part of her story. It underscores her remarkable strength and resilience, her determination to rise above her circumstances and reclaim her life. It's a story that has resonated with countless others who have faced similar battles, inspiring them with the message that it's possible to break free from the cycle of abuse.

Tina Turner's legacy extends beyond her illustrious music career. She is a beacon of hope, a symbol of triumph over adversity. By sharing her experiences, she has helped bring the issue of domestic violence out of the shadows, giving voice to those who, like herself, have suffered in silence.

The unseen battles Tina fought within her marriage to Ike were undoubtedly some of the toughest challenges she faced. Yet, they forged an integral part of the resilient, courageous woman the world came to adore. Her story stands testament to the fact that no matter the trials we face, it's possible to overcome them and emerge stronger, just like Tina did. As we remember her life and her music, let's also remember her strength, courage, and indomitable spirit that truly made her "Simply the Best".

# Moment Nr. 14

## *Independence Day: The brave night she left Ike in Dallas, 1976*

The year was 1976, and in Dallas, Texas, an event transpired that marked a turning point in Tina Turner's life. In a bold, life-altering decision, she summoned the courage to walk away from an oppressive, 16-year-long marriage to Ike Turner. This night was not just about escaping an abusive relationship; it was about reclaiming her life, her identity, and her freedom. This was Tina's Independence Day.

The Ike & Tina Turner Revue had brought them fame and recognition, but the glittering façade concealed a harrowing truth. The price Tina paid for her success was a life marked by constant control, fear, and physical abuse. She lived a life that was miles away from the flamboyant, energetic performer who captivated audiences worldwide.

July 1st, 1976, was the night when Tina, having suffered a particularly brutal altercation with Ike, decided that enough was enough. Despite the fear, despite the uncertainty of what lay ahead, she chose to step into the unknown. Armed only with a Mobil credit card and a courageous spirit, she left the hotel they were staying at, running across a freeway to find sanctuary.

This decision to leave Ike was a monumental step for Tina. It was more than an act of self-preservation; it was an assertion of her worth and a rejection of the life she had been coerced into. She chose uncertainty and struggle over continuing the cycle of abuse, a testament to her resilience and indomitable spirit.

The aftermath was far from easy. Tina had to rebuild her life from scratch, often performing in smaller venues, dealing with legal battles, and facing financial difficulties. But through it all, she persisted. Tina's journey wasn't just about the pursuit of a successful solo career; it was about discovering her voice, her strength, and above all, her self-worth.

Tina Turner's Independence Day was a seminal moment that defined her life and career. Her decision to break free from her abusive marriage, though fraught with challenges, paved the way for her to become the global music sensation we remember today. She didn't just survive; she thrived, reaching heights that few could have envisioned.

The brave night Tina left Ike serves as a beacon of hope, not just for those trapped in abusive relationships, but for anyone facing adversity. It symbolizes the power of courage, the importance of self-worth, and the unyielding belief in one's ability to change their circumstances.

Remembering Tina Turner is about celebrating her talent, her music, her passion. But it's equally about acknowledging her strength, her courage, and her resilience. She stands as a testament to the power of resilience, and her Independence Day remains a pivotal moment in her life – a moment when she chose herself, chose freedom, and ultimately, chose life.

From Nutbush's small-town girl to the queen of rock 'n' roll, Tina Turner's journey is a powerful narrative of resilience and transformation. It is a story of how one woman, against all odds, stood up for herself, refusing to be defined by her circumstances, making her, truly, "Simply the Best".

# Moment Nr. 15

## *The Start of a Solo Career: Overcoming Hurdles and Critics*

When Tina Turner left her tumultuous marriage to Ike in 1976, she stepped into an uncertain future. Having been part of the Ike & Tina Turner Revue for nearly two decades, venturing solo into the music world posed an uphill battle. Nevertheless, Turner's spirit, forged by a lifetime of resilience, was unyielding. Her pursuit of a solo career became a testament to her tenacity, marking the dawn of a new era in her life.

Armed with her stage name, a Mobil credit card, and an unshakeable determination, Tina set about rebuilding her life and career from scratch. Initially, the journey was fraught with financial difficulties and legal battles, exacerbated by skeptics who believed her time in the spotlight had passed. Yet, undeterred by the barrage of challenges, Tina remained resolute, finding work in cabarets and TV appearances to support herself and her children.

Through these years, Tina nurtured her craft, honing her unique style and proving her mettle as a versatile performer. From rock 'n' roll to soul and pop, her range was impressive, showcasing the raw, fiery energy that she became renowned for. By 1984, nearly eight years after her brave escape, Tina's breakthrough came with the release of her album, 'Private Dancer'. The album was a roaring success, transforming her from a has-been to a solo superstar almost overnight. The girl from Nutbush had reemerged, fiercer and more triumphant than ever.

'Private Dancer' not only revived her career but it also restored her confidence and belief in her abilities. Its chart-topping tracks like "What's Love Got To Do With It" and "Better Be Good To Me" resonated with millions of fans, earning Tina three Grammy Awards. This marked a monumental triumph over the skeptics who had doubted her ability to revive her career.

Tina's journey to solo stardom was not just about professional success; it was a personal victory, an affirmation of her indomitable spirit. It demonstrated her capacity to rise from the ashes, to reclaim her place in the music industry, and above all, to redefine herself independent of Ike. It was a testament to her unwavering resilience, a trait that would define her throughout her life and career.

Tina Turner's solo career is a captivating story of overcoming odds. It reminds us that no hurdle is too high, no critic too daunting, and no past too binding for those who dare to dream and persist. It is about celebrating the strength and courage it took for one woman to confront her fears, chase her dreams, and finally, to stand on her own.

In the tale of Tina Turner, we celebrate not just a global music sensation, but a woman of resilience, courage, and strength. From her small-town roots to her solo stardom, her journey is a testament to the power of self-belief, perseverance, and sheer determination. And for this reason, and so many others, Tina Turner will always be remembered as "Simply the Best".

# PART 05: The Solo Comeback

# Moment Nr. 16

## *Rough Beginnings: The Struggle to get back on her feet after Separating from Ike*

Born Anna Mae Bullock in the humble town of Nutbush, Tennessee, the future Queen of Rock 'n' Roll, Tina Turner, endured a tumultuous journey. Her struggle to regain her footing after a tumultuous relationship with Ike Turner proved to be one of the most defining periods in her life.

In 1976, having endured a marriage riddled with abuse and humiliation, Tina made the life-altering decision to escape from Ike, taking nothing but her stage name and a sense of unyielding determination. This marked the birth of her solo career, a momentous occasion as significant as her own birth. It was not just the genesis of an artist; it was the rebirth of a woman who refused to be a victim.

Yet, the path was far from easy. Devoid of financial resources and burdened with debt, Tina faced daunting hurdles. Her name, associated with the 'Ike & Tina Turner Revue', held a dual-edged significance. While it gave her a platform in the music industry, it also tied her to an abusive past. Many promoters were skeptical about her viability as a solo act. Nevertheless, she braved the challenges, showing the world the tenacity behind her dazzling smile.

Tina found herself performing in small venues, cabarets, and TV shows to make ends meet. The contrast between her past as a celebrated artist and her current struggle was stark, but her spirit remained unbroken. She drew strength from these rough beginnings, turning her struggles into a powerful narrative that resonated with her audience.

Moreover, Tina's faith in Buddhism fueled her strength and determination. The philosophy of turning poison into medicine became a core tenet of her life. Her hardships were not obstacles; they were stepping stones propelling her toward a triumphant future.

Slowly, Tina began to redefine her musical identity. She collaborated with different musicians, explored various genres, and ultimately established herself as a versatile solo artist. Her unique blend of rock 'n' roll, R&B, and pop music, paired with her electrifying performances, soon caught the attention of the public and critics alike.

Tina's rough beginnings were not a phase of failure; they were a period of resilience and growth. She stood tall against adversity, reaffirming her belief in herself and her dreams. This part of her life was a testament to her immense strength, highlighting her rise from the ashes like a phoenix. It reflected the unyielding spirit of a woman who dared to defy the odds and rebuild her life from scratch.

This phase of Tina Turner's life was pivotal, not only to her career but also to millions of fans worldwide. Her struggle was a source of inspiration, a beacon of hope that resonated with people facing their battles. In her story, they saw a reflection of their struggles and the possibility of triumph.

"Rough Beginnings" is more than just a subchapter in Tina Turner's life. It is a testament to the indomitable spirit of a woman born in a small town who soared to global stardom. The hardships she faced after her separation from Ike became the foundation of her solo career, proving to the world that Tina Turner was, indeed, "Simply the Best".

# Moment Nr. 17

## *The Second Time Around: Recording her Cover of "Let's Stay Together"*

When you think of Anna Mae Bullock, the dynamo from Nutbush, Tennessee who would come to be known as Tina Turner, it's impossible not to acknowledge her profound journey of reinvention. One of the most pivotal moments in her solo career came in 1983 when she recorded a sultry, rock-infused cover of Al Green's "Let's Stay Together," a song that set the stage for her explosive return to the mainstream music scene.

Having navigated the turbulent waters of her post-Ike Turner life, Tina was primed to redefine her musical career. However, with the image of 'Ike & Tina' still prevalent in many minds, a successful comeback required a daring move. It was her rendition of "Let's Stay Together" that became that audacious step, marking her rebirth as a solo artist.

The decision to cover this classic was not without its risks. The original was a cherished soul hit, and the idea of reinterpreting it in a rock and pop vein could have been met with resistance. Yet, it was Tina's ability to take this risk, to breathe new life into the song with her unique interpretation, that made the cover so extraordinary.

Tina poured her heart into the recording, filling every note with the raw emotion of her journey. The result was an electrifying blend of soulful lyrics and rock 'n' roll energy, a song that was undeniably Tina. It not only captivated listeners but also introduced Tina Turner to a new generation of fans.

Her rendition of "Let's Stay Together" became an international hit, propelling her into the limelight once again. It marked the beginning of her ascension to global stardom, an ascent filled with multiple chart-topping hits, sold-out concerts, and awards. More importantly, it symbolized the triumph of her indomitable spirit.

Every note she sang on "Let's Stay Together" was a testament to her resilience. Here was a woman who had weathered the worst of storms, emerging not as a victim, but a victor. She transformed her pain into art, her struggles into a melody that echoed around the world.

Tina Turner's cover of "Let's Stay Together" is a milestone in her career. It reflects the essence of her journey - the tenacity to rise above adversity, the courage to reinvent oneself, and the audacity to do so in a public sphere. This recording did more than revitalize her career; it sent a powerful message of endurance and strength.

In the world of music and beyond, Tina Turner remains a beacon of hope and a symbol of resilience. She navigated her career and personal life with grace and grit, transforming every obstacle into a stepping-stone. The same girl from Nutbush who transformed into a global sensation continues to inspire millions through her life and music. As we remember Tina, her rendition of "Let's Stay Together" stands as a triumphant anthem of her remarkable journey, a testament to her enduring spirit and extraordinary talent.

# Moment Nr. 18

## *The Private Dancer Album: Behind the Scenes of her major Comeback*

The annals of music history are filled with triumphant comebacks, but none are as compelling and inspiring as Tina Turner's in 1984 with the release of "Private Dancer." This seminal album is a testament to Turner's resilience and her inimitable talent, a sonic landscape that catapulted her back onto the world stage and firmly into the hearts of millions.

Following her successful cover of "Let's Stay Together," the anticipation for Tina's next move was palpable. Her partnership with Capitol Records and the support from manager Roger Davies set the stage for a project that would redefine her career. "Private Dancer" was more than just an album; it was a statement, a proclamation of her liberation and strength.

The album was a bold departure from her previous work. It was here that Tina truly found her groove, intertwining her rock roots with elements of pop, soul, and dance. She took charge, showcasing her versatility and creative range. Each track was imbued with her unique vocal prowess, the emotive grit of her voice narrating stories of love, pain, and triumph.

Songs like "What's Love Got to Do with It" and "Better Be Good to Me" resonated with listeners, transforming Tina into a symbol of female empowerment. However, it was the title track, "Private Dancer," that offered a deeper insight into her soul. The song unveiled a more vulnerable side of Tina, an intimate portrayal of the woman behind the powerhouse.

Recording "Private Dancer" was no small feat. Tina put her heart and soul into every track, her determination and commitment mirrored in the long hours she spent in the studio. It was this unwavering dedication that shone through every note, a testament to her unyielding spirit and tenacity.

On its release, "Private Dancer" was met with widespread critical acclaim, a commercial success that marked Tina's indisputable comeback. The album sold millions of copies worldwide, spawned multiple hit singles, and won her several prestigious awards, including three Grammys. But beyond its commercial success, "Private Dancer" was a personal victory for Tina.

"Private Dancer" was more than just a collection of songs; it was an affirmation of Tina's resilience, a tangible product of her newfound freedom. The album stood as an emblem of her victory over past adversities, a triumphant declaration that Tina Turner was back, and she was stronger than ever.

In a career spanning over six decades, Tina Turner has left an indelible imprint on the music industry and beyond. From her humble beginnings in Nutbush to her meteoric rise to global stardom, her journey is a testament to the enduring spirit of determination and resilience. As we celebrate her life and legacy, "Private Dancer" remains a symbol of her strength, a reminder that even in the face of adversity, Tina Turner remained 'simply the best.'

# Moment Nr. 19

## *What's Love Got to Do with It? The Unexpected Success of this Solo Single*

The year was 1984, and the question on everybody's lips was, "What's Love Got to Do with It?" The infectious rhythm and poignant lyrics of this iconic Tina Turner single swept across radio waves, resonating in the hearts of listeners worldwide. This powerful track, a key component of her comeback album "Private Dancer," marked a transformative point in Tina's career and left a deep imprint on popular music culture.

The story behind the song is one of fate and a testament to Tina's exceptional intuition. Initially, she wasn't particularly enthusiastic about recording it. She considered it to be too 'pop' and not sufficiently aligned with her rock and soul roots. However, her manager Roger Davies and the songwriters Terry Britten and Graham Lyle convinced her to give it a shot. And thus, a legendary tune was born.

When Tina stepped into the studio, she infused every note with her unique charisma, imbuing the track with a raw emotion that transcended the original composition. Her voice, gritty yet soulful, breathed life into the lyrics, transforming them into a poignant exploration of love and relationships. It was this authentic emotional connection that endeared the song to her fans, propelling it to the top of the charts.

To the world's surprise, "What's Love Got to Do with It" skyrocketed to the number one spot on the Billboard Hot 100, holding its position for three weeks. It was her first significant American hit as a solo artist, a testament to her ability to connect with a broader audience. The song's popularity ushered in a wave of critical acclaim, leading to a Grammy win for Record of the Year and Best Female Pop Vocal Performance in 1985.

But beyond its commercial success, "What's Love Got to Do with It" held a deeper significance. The song marked a pivotal moment in Tina's journey, symbolizing her liberation from past challenges and her reclamation of personal and artistic control. It was more than just a hit single; it was a testament to her endurance, talent, and the power of transformation.

The success of "What's Love Got to Do with It" propelled Tina to unprecedented heights, firmly re-establishing her position in the music industry. But more importantly, it gave her a platform to share her story, inspiring millions worldwide with her resilience and indomitable spirit.

The magic of Tina Turner isn't just found in her powerful vocals or her electrifying performances. It's in her capacity to rise above adversity, to rebuild and reinvent herself continually. As we remember Tina Turner, we don't just celebrate a global music sensation; we honor a woman whose extraordinary life journey resonates with hope, resilience, and the unfaltering belief that love, indeed, has everything to do with it.

# Moment Nr. 20

---

## *The Unforgettable Grammy Night: The evening she took home four Grammy Awards*

In the annals of music history, few comeback stories shine as brightly as Tina Turner's. After a career fraught with tumult, Tina embarked on a solo journey in the early 1980s that would lead her to heights she hadn't seen before. It was a journey marked by determination, resilience, and an unwavering belief in her own talent. The pinnacle of this journey was reached on February 26, 1985, a night that would forever remain etched in the annals of Grammy history.

On this night, Tina Turner, the girl from Nutbush, Tennessee, stood in the spotlight on the Grammy stage, basking in the glory that was a testament to her remarkable talent and tenacity. Tina, who had recently released her triumphant album "Private Dancer," was about to make Grammy history.

The evening kicked off with Tina's gripping performance of "What's Love Got to Do with It," a track from "Private Dancer" that had propelled her back into the limelight the previous year. Dressed in a shimmering silver dress, Tina commanded the stage with an electrifying presence that was nothing short of mesmerizing. The applause that followed her performance was deafening, a resounding affirmation of her enduring talent.

As the evening progressed, the magnitude of Tina's triumph became clear. She won four Grammy Awards – Record of the Year, Best Female Pop Vocal Performance, Best Female Rock Vocal Performance, and Best Rock Performance by a Duo or Group with Vocal. Each award was a symbol of her resilience, a recognition of her remarkable talent, and a tribute to her exceptional comeback.

"What's Love Got to Do with It," a song that Tina had initially been skeptical about, won two awards. Tina had transformed the song with her distinct style, turning it into an anthem of independence that resonated with millions around the globe. The song was not just a hit; it was a reflection of Tina's own journey towards self-love and self-respect.

Her victory in the Best Female Rock Vocal Performance category highlighted Tina's prowess as a versatile artist and her undeniable impact on the realm of rock 'n' roll. But it was perhaps the award for Best Rock Performance by a Duo or Group with Vocal, which Tina shared with her producer, Rupert Hine, for "Better Be Good to Me," that held the most significance. This award was a testament to Tina's triumph over her past and a symbol of her victorious comeback.

That unforgettable Grammy night was a milestone in Tina Turner's life and career. It marked her re-emergence as a music superstar and symbolized her victory over adversity. Today, as we remember Tina Turner, we celebrate not just her immense talent but also her indomitable spirit and her unwavering resilience.

From Nutbush to the Grammy stage, Tina Turner's journey is a testament to her enduring legacy. As we commemorate her life, we celebrate the remarkable journey of a woman who truly was 'Simply the Best.'

# PART 06: Triumph and Recognition

# Moment Nr. 21

## *Mad Max: The impact of her role in Mad Max Beyond Thunderdome*

Every journey has its unexpected twists and turns, and Tina Turner's was no exception. Born Anna Mae Bullock on November 26, 1939, Tina began her journey in the humble town of Nutbush, Tennessee, and charted a path that would lead her to become a musical icon. Yet, in 1985, a new venture beckoned that would forever mark her legacy - her role in the movie "Mad Max Beyond Thunderdome."

Tina, already recognized as a musical powerhouse, was cast as the audacious 'Aunty Entity,' the ruler of Bartertown. This was a significant shift from her established career in music, but as ever, Tina rose to the challenge.

Her role in "Mad Max Beyond Thunderdome" was an embodiment of her spirit. Just as Tina had challenged norms in her musical career, Aunty Entity defied expectations in the apocalyptic world of Mad Max. She was fierce, powerful, and indomitable, traits that Tina herself personified in real life.

Beyond her acting, Tina also contributed to the film's electrifying soundtrack, performing "We Don't Need Another Hero (Thunderdome)" and "One of the Living." Both songs resonated with her personal narrative of resilience and strength, amplifying the impact of the film and further solidifying Tina's legendary status.

"We Don't Need Another Hero (Thunderdome)" was an immediate hit. The song, like Tina, was a beacon of resilience, echoing the film's themes of survival and tenacity. It became a global success, reaching the top of the charts in several countries and earning Tina a Grammy nomination.

Tina's role in Mad Max was more than just an acting gig – it was an extension of her own life, echoing her journey from Nutbush to global stardom. Through Aunty Entity, Tina projected a powerful image of female strength and leadership, which resonated with audiences worldwide.

The success of the film and her contributions to its soundtrack brought Tina a new level of recognition and added another layer to her multi-faceted career. "Mad Max Beyond Thunderdome" show-cased Tina Turner as not just a singer, but an actress and a powerful storyteller, adding another string to her already impressive bow.

Tina's foray into acting also proved that she was not one to be confined by expectations. She embraced the challenge of a new medium, demonstrating the versatility that would become a hall-mark of her career. Just as she had transcended musical genres, she seamlessly transitioned into acting, winning over audiences and critics alike.

As we remember Tina Turner, we celebrate not just her extraordinary musical journey, but also her impactful venture into acting. With her role in "Mad Max Beyond Thunderdome," Tina showed the world that she was more than just a music icon – she was a versatile, fearless artist willing to explore new frontiers and blaze her own trail. Her performance in the film remains a testa-ment to her unyielding spirit, reminding us that Tina Turner was, indeed, simply the best.

# Moment Nr. 22

## Her Autobiography 'I, Tina': Revealing her story to the world

From her humble beginnings in Nutbush, Tennessee, Tina Turner's journey was a testament to the enduring human spirit. Born Anna Mae Bullock on November 26, 1939, Tina Turner's transformative journey is a powerful tale of resilience and tenacity.

In 1986, Tina decided it was time to share her truth with the world, collaborating with Kurt Loder to pen her autobiography, 'I, Tina.' This moment was pivotal not only for Tina but for the millions of fans who admired her. For the first time, fans would get a glimpse into Tina's world beyond the stage lights and fanfare.

'I, Tina' was more than just a retelling of Tina's journey to stardom; it was an honest, heart-wrenching account of her struggles and triumphs. Tina didn't shy away from the difficult parts of her life. From her tumultuous marriage to Ike Turner to her hard-fought journey to solo stardom, 'I, Tina' was a raw, authentic, and intimate look at the woman behind the legend.

'I, Tina' showcased her exceptional courage and strength, offering a firsthand account of how she found the fortitude to escape an abusive marriage and re-establish herself as a successful solo artist.

It was an ode to her indomitable spirit, a testament to her perseverance. This powerful narrative resonated deeply with readers worldwide, allowing them to connect with Tina on a profoundly personal level.

But the book was not just about struggle; it was also a celebration of her incredible journey in the music industry. It provided insight into the making of her iconic hits and gave readers a taste of the electric energy that infused her live performances. 'I, Tina' showcased her infectious spirit, her unyielding passion for music, and her dedication to her craft.

This revealing autobiography served as an inspiration for many. Through her personal narrative, Tina sent a powerful message about resilience, self-reliance, and the importance of never giving up, no matter how insurmountable the odds seem.


'I, Tina' wasn't merely a story; it was a testament to a woman's unyielding strength and an enduring symbol of resilience and self-belief. With 'I, Tina', the legendary artist opened up her world, allowing us to understand the trials, tribulations, and triumphs that shaped the Queen of Rock 'n' Roll.

The impact of 'I, Tina' was immense. It laid the foundation for the 1993 biopic 'What's Love Got to Do with It,' which further introduced Tina's life and career to a broader audience. Both the book and the film contributed significantly to Tina's legacy, solidifying her place as a powerful symbol of strength and perseverance.

As we celebrate Tina Turner's life, we must remember the significance of 'I, Tina'. In telling her story, Tina showed us that we too could overcome adversity. Her life served as a powerful lesson in resilience, one that will continue to inspire millions for generations to come.

In the end, 'I, Tina' was not just an autobiography; it was a love letter to life itself, a testament to the power of perseverance, and a celebration of a woman who rose from humble beginnings to become a global icon. Through 'I, Tina', we remember and celebrate the life of Tina Turner, a woman who was, indeed, 'Simply the Best.'

# Moment Nr. 23

---

## *Tina's Big Screen Biopic: The making of 'What's Love Got to Do with It'*

It was November 26, 1939, when the rural town of Nutbush, Tennessee, welcomed into the world a baby girl destined to become one of the most influential voices in music. Anna Mae Bullock, who we would later come to know as Tina Turner, entered a world far removed from the glittering stages and roaring crowds that would one day become her reality. But Tina's story was not one of overnight success. It was a tale of triumph born from adversity, a narrative woven through the fabric of her unforgettable music and her indomitable spirit.

Fast-forward to 1993, the world was granted an intimate look into the journey that transformed Anna Mae Bullock into the beloved Tina Turner. "What's Love Got to Do with It," a cinematic testament to her rise, resilience, and redemption, shone a light on her life like never before. This biopic was a game-changer not just for Tina, but also for the millions who adored her.

Adapting such a monumental life to the silver screen was no mean feat. But under the masterful direction of Brian Gibson and with Angela Bassett embodying Tina with her exceptional portrayal, the film emerged as an unforgettable, honest tribute to the Queen of Rock 'n' Roll.

Just like Tina herself, the film pulled no punches. It was a raw and often painful narrative, revealing her turbulent relationship with Ike Turner, portrayed by Laurence Fishburne. Yet, as difficult as these moments were to watch, they were crucial in painting a vivid picture of Tina's tenacity. It highlighted the incredible strength it took for her to escape the confines of her personal turmoil and build a solo career that eventually outshone her past.

Beyond the gritty drama, the film was also a celebration of Tina's musical genius. From the intimate moments in the studio to the electrifying performances on stage, it captured the infectious energy and sheer talent that Tina exuded. Every beat, every note was an homage to her enduring legacy.

The making of "What's Love Got to Do with It" was not simply about recounting Tina's past. It was about drawing inspiration from her struggles, her victories, and her spirit. For many, the film served as a beacon of resilience, a testament to the power of perseverance. Tina Turner, with her life laid bare on celluloid, became a beacon for those navigating their storms.

While the film garnered critical acclaim and numerous awards, including an Oscar nomination for Bassett, its greatest triumph lay in the resonance of Tina's story. Her trials, her grit, her resurgence echoed through the narrative, reminding everyone that life, in all its highs and lows, is a song worth singing.

Tina Turner wasn't just a rock legend; she was a trailblazer who carved her own path, a warrior who rose above adversity, and a queen who, through her music and life, taught us what it truly meant to be "Simply the Best." Through "What's Love Got to Do with It," we witnessed the making of this queen, a heart-rending and heart-warming journey that continues to inspire.

From the humble beginnings in Nutbush to the gleaming lights of global stardom, Tina Turner's story was a symphony of resilience, redemption, and unyielding strength. As we revisit the making of her biopic, we pay tribute to the woman behind the legend, acknowledging her not just as an icon, but as a beacon of strength, an embodiment of tenacity, and a testament to the enduring power of the human spirit.

# Moment Nr. 24

## The 50th Anniversary Tour: Celebrating five Decades in Music

Five decades of extraordinary music-making. Five decades of electrifying performances. Five decades of the indomitable Tina Turner. On November 26, 1939, in the humble town of Nutbush, Tennessee, a star was born who would illuminate the world of music like few others.

Fast forward to 2008, when Tina Turner, at the age of 68, embarked on her 50th Anniversary Tour – a milestone moment that signified not just a celebration of her monumental career, but also her unwavering resilience, her infectious spirit, and her unyielding passion for music.

The "Tina!: 50th Anniversary Tour" was, in every sense, a testament to the transformative power of music and the iconic woman at its heart. With Tina having officially retired from performing in 2000, this tour was a triumphant return, a gift to the fans who had adored her music and revered her journey for five decades.

From the moment she took the stage, it was evident that Tina Turner had lost none of her magic. The energy was electric, her voice, just as powerful and soulful as ever, echoed through the venues. Every performance was an exhibition of her unmatchable talent, her tenacious spirit, and her lifelong dedication to her craft.

Yet, it was more than just a series of concerts. This tour was an embodiment of Tina's enduring legacy – a tangible, exhilarating celebration of a journey filled with triumphs and trials. It was a nostalgic journey down memory lane for many, a chance to relive the hits that had become anthems, from "Private Dancer" to "What's Love Got to Do with It."

Seeing Tina on stage again was a powerful reminder of her incredible journey, a celebration of a woman who rose from a small-town girl to an international icon. Her performances served as an embodiment of her strength and tenacity, her relentless determination to conquer every challenge and emerge stronger, better, and more dedicated to her music.

For Tina, the 50th Anniversary Tour was a celebration of resilience. It was a testament to her enduring love for music and her fans. It was about embracing her age, her legacy, and her iconic status, proving that passion, talent, and perseverance know no bounds.

The tour was a resounding success, both critically and commercially, proving yet again that Tina Turner was indeed 'Simply the Best.' But beyond its success, the tour represented something far more significant. It was a celebration of a woman who had defied odds, broken barriers, and transformed the world of music with her soulful voice and indomitable spirit.

As we commemorate Tina's 50th Anniversary Tour, we remember not just an unforgettable series of performances but a tribute to a life lived in the glare of the spotlight, a life dedicated to the pursuit of musical excellence. We remember Tina Turner, the resilient woman who rose from the small town of Nutbush, Tennessee, to become a global phenomenon, a beacon of strength, and a true icon.

From her humble beginnings to her triumphant 50th-anniversary tour, Tina Turner's story remains a testament to the human spirit's power, a symphony of resilience, and an enduring inspiration for generations. In celebrating her life and career, we honor the woman behind the legend, recognizing her as not only an iconic musician but as a symbol of strength, tenacity, and ceaseless passion for her craft.

# PART 07: Later Life and Legacy

# Moment Nr. 25

## *A Love Story: Her Relationship and later Marriage to Erwin Bach*

In the midst of Tina Turner's whirlwind life filled with music, performances, and personal trials, there emerged a love story as compelling and powerful as the legendary artist herself. A love story with a man named Erwin Bach, who would become not just her partner, but her rock in the years to come.

Erwin Bach, a German music executive, met Tina in 1985 at an EMI record label party in London. The attraction was mutual and immediate. Tina, then 46, and Bach, 16 years her junior, began a relationship that would soon become a rock of stability in Tina's life. They were two individuals from vastly different worlds, yet they found in each other a mutual understanding and admiration that would blossom into profound love.

Their relationship was not one characterized by the flamboyance and spectacle often associated with the music industry. Instead, it was a relationship built on respect, companionship, and an under-stated, yet deep love. They moved together to Switzerland in 1994, choosing a life of privacy and tranquillity away from the glaring spotlight of fame.

In the years that followed, Bach became not just Tina's partner, but also her confidante, her pillar of strength. In the tumultuous sea that was Tina's life, Bach was her harbor, providing her with the love and stability that had often eluded her in the past. For Tina, Bach was a symbol of her triumphant journey towards love and self-worth, proof that after years of hardship, she could find and embrace love.

After 27 years of unwavering companionship, Tina and Bach tied the knot in a private ceremony on the shores of Lake Zurich in 2013. The wedding was a reflection of their love – simple, authentic, and deeply personal. Tina, the queen of rock 'n' roll, adorned in a green and black silk Armani gown, exchanged vows with Bach, marking the beginning of a new chapter in their love story.

Their marriage, however, was more a testament of their bond than a change in their relationship. Tina would often say that she and Bach had felt married long before they made it official. Their wedding was merely a celebration of the love that they had nurtured and shared over the years.

As we remember Tina Turner, it's essential to acknowledge the role Erwin Bach played in her life. Their love story serves as a poignant reminder that behind the iconic artist was a woman who sought love, companionship, and stability. A woman who, in the twilight of her life, found these in a love story that was as compelling and inspiring as her remarkable journey.

In celebrating Tina Turner's life, we celebrate not just her music, her triumphs, and her resilience. We also celebrate her love story with Erwin Bach, a testament to the enduring power of love in the face of adversity. A testament that indeed, love had everything to do with it.

# Moment Nr. 26

## *The Spiritual Journey: The Influence of Buddhism on Her Life*

Throughout her tumultuous and remarkable life, Tina Turner found solace, strength, and resilience in a somewhat unexpected source: the spiritual practices of Buddhism. In the whirlwind of her incredible journey, Buddhism was not just a peripheral influence; it became an essential core of Tina's life, guiding her through hardships and triumphs alike.

Tina was introduced to Buddhism in the early 1970s amidst a tumultuous period of her life. It was then, during the most challenging moments, that she found solace in the teachings of Nichiren Buddhism. The core practice of chanting "Nam Myoho Renge Kyo" became a beacon of hope, a source of resilience, and a pathway to inner peace.

The power of this chant, translated as "I devote myself to the Mystic Law of the Lotus Sutra," held a profound significance for Tina. In her own words, it meant awakening her life's potential, transforming her destiny, and ultimately, gaining the strength to survive and thrive amidst adversity. In the raw rhythm of this chant, Tina found a powerful echo of her own voice—a voice that could conquer fear, pain, and self-doubt.

Incorporating Buddhism into her life was more than adopting a new belief system. For Tina, it became a pathway to empowerment and self-understanding. It was a compass guiding her to navigate life's storms, an anchor amidst turbulent waters. It was a philosophy that centered on the idea of 'human revolution,' a concept that echoed her own transformative journey from hardship to global success.

Moreover, Buddhism taught Tina the power of resilience and the limitless potential within her own life. It inspired her to forge her path, to overcome adversity, and to create a life defined not by circumstances but by her indomitable spirit. And in doing so, Tina became a beacon of inspiration herself, her life story a testament to the transformative power of faith and resilience.


In her later years, Tina would often speak of her spiritual journey, reflecting on the profound impact Buddhism had on her life. She would describe the sense of peace she found in chanting, the strength it offered her, and the perspective it provided.

As we celebrate Tina Turner's extraordinary life, it is crucial to recognize the profound influence Buddhism had on her journey. For in understanding her spiritual path, we gain a deeper appreciation of the strength, resilience, and inner peace that marked her remarkable journey. We come to understand a side of Tina that perhaps resonated most deeply with her—the side that found strength in spirituality, power in faith, and resilience in the rhythm of a chant.

The spiritual journey of Tina Turner reminds us that amid life's storms, we can find an inner sanctuary of peace and resilience. And in doing so, we celebrate Tina not just as a legendary performer, but also as a spiritual beacon—an emblem of strength, resilience, and unwavering faith.

In Tina's own words, "I didn't have anybody, really, no foundation in life, so I had to make my own way. Always, from the start. I had to go out in the world and become strong, to discover my mission in life." Buddhism was a significant part of this mission, a guiding light that illuminated her path and shone brightly in her heart.

# Moment Nr. 27

## *The Farewell: Her Reasons for Bidding Goodbye to Concert Tours*

There comes a point in every performer's life when the glare of the spotlights, the roar of the crowd, and the adrenaline of the concert stage give way to a longing for peace, quiet, and simplicity. For Tina Turner, an unparalleled force in music, that moment arrived after a career that spanned over half a century. The Farewell Tour, as it was aptly named, was her goodbye to concert tours, but far from a retreat, it marked the beginning of a new chapter in her life.

Tina had always lived life at full throttle. From her humble beginnings in Nutbush, Tennessee, to the dazzling heights of international stardom, she had not merely survived; she had thrived, turning adversity into fuel for success. Yet, after years of electrifying performances and constant touring, Tina began to yearn for a change.

In her 2005 autobiography 'I, Tina: My Life Story,' Tina stated that the grueling demands of life on the road had started to take a toll on her. She felt a growing desire to slow down, to experience life away from the relentless pace of tours and performances. More than anything, she wanted to embrace a simpler lifestyle, one that would afford her the luxury of time—time for herself, her loved ones, and the serenity she craved.

A significant factor in Tina's decision was her enduring love for Erwin Bach, whom she had met in 1985 and married in 2013. Their relationship, a sanctuary amidst the whirlwind of her career, provided the emotional support she needed. With Bach by her side, the prospect of stepping away from the public eye became not just feasible but attractive.

And so, in 2000, Tina embarked on her Twenty-Four Seven Tour, a series of concerts that were to be her swan song to the world of live performance. She took to the stage with the same fiery passion and unflagging energy that had characterized her career, but this time, it was tinged with the bittersweet knowledge that this was her farewell.

Her reasons for bidding goodbye to concert tours were deeply personal, rooted in a need for balance and peace. But in true Tina Turner fashion, her farewell was not a quiet retreat—it was a blaze of glory, a testament to her indomitable spirit.

Tina Turner's farewell to concert tours is a reminder that every end is merely a new beginning. As she left the concert stage, she embraced a new phase of life with the same passion and tenacity that had driven her extraordinary career. Her journey reminds us that it's never too late to change course, to prioritize our well-being, and to seek out the life we truly want.

As we celebrate the life of Tina Turner, her farewell tour stands as an enduring symbol of her courage, her resilience, and her unwavering dedication to living life on her own terms. And in doing so, she proved once again why she will always be Simply the Best.

# Moment Nr. 28

## Tina the Musical: The Stage Production That Honors Her Legacy

Long after the echoes of Tina Turner's final farewell to concert tours had faded, her life and music took center stage once again in "Tina - The Tina Turner Musical." This critically acclaimed stage production was not just a celebration of Tina's music, but a tribute to her indomitable spirit, her courage, and her journey of transformation.

From her birth in a small segregated town in Tennessee to the towering heights of global stardom, Tina's life was a tapestry of triumphs and trials, resilience and reinvention. The musical encapsulates this journey in an inspiring narrative accompanied by the unforgettable music that was her life's soundtrack. Every chord struck, every line delivered, serves as a testament to Tina's exceptional life and career.

"Tina - The Tina Turner Musical" debuted in London's West End in 2018, a gift to a world that could never get enough of the Queen of Rock 'n' Roll. Tina, personally involved in the production, lent her insights, ensuring that the story portrayed on stage mirrored her lived experience. This authenticity shone through, creating an immersive and deeply moving experience for the audience.

The musical did not shy away from the darker parts of her journey, but faced them head-on, mirroring Tina's own courage. From her tumultuous relationship with Ike Turner to her inspiring comeback in the 80s, every chapter of her life was laid bare, celebrated in all its raw and unvarnished truth.

The show's success was indisputable, enjoying rave reviews and packed houses. It quickly became a testament to Tina's enduring appeal, long after she had stepped away from the public eye. In 2019, the show hit Broadway, reaching an even wider audience and cementing Tina's legacy in the annals of popular culture.

More than a tribute, "Tina - The Tina Turner Musical" is a living testament to her journey. It portrays not just the superstar but the woman behind the legend - her struggles, her triumphs, and above all, her humanity. By showcasing her life and music, the musical serves as a powerful reminder of the resilience of the human spirit and the transformative power of music.

The significance of "Tina - The Tina Turner Musical" extends beyond its immediate success. It serves as a beacon, shining a light on Tina's life and legacy, ensuring that her story continues to inspire future generations. Just as Tina Turner once set the music world ablaze with her talent and charisma, her story continues to ignite the stage, a testament to her lasting impact on music and culture.

From her humble beginnings to her reign as the Queen of Rock 'n' Roll, Tina Turner's journey has been nothing short of extraordinary. As we remember and celebrate her life, "Tina - The Tina Turner Musical" stands as a testament to her enduring legacy, a shining tribute to a life that truly was "Simply the Best."

# Moment Nr. 29

## *Iconic Tina: The Significant Influence of Her Unique Style and Sound on the Music Industry*

There are few figures in music who have managed to alter the landscape as dramatically as Tina Turner. Her music, a vibrant amalgamation of soul, rock 'n' roll, and pop, presented a unique sound that both thrilled and intrigued. Her style, both on stage and off, was daringly unique, earning her not just fans but followers, transforming the course of music.

Born in Nutbush, Tennessee, Tina's journey to stardom was far from straightforward. Her early years were marked by hardship, but also by a deep-rooted love of music. It was this love that ultimately propelled her into a career that would span over half a century, touching the lives of millions worldwide.

Tina's sound was distinctive – a combination of soulful R&B, raw rock, and infectious pop that transcended genre boundaries. From her earlier hits with Ike Turner like "Proud Mary," to her solo triumphs such as "What's Love Got To Do With It," Tina's music exhibited a versatility and depth that resonated with a diverse range of audiences.

What set Tina apart, however, was not just her music but the persona that infused it. Her performances were high-voltage spectacles of energy, each one a testament to her unrivaled stamina and presence. Her distinct voice, raspy yet powerful, filled each song with a palpable emotion that audiences connected with. Tina Turner was not merely a singer – she was a force of nature, electrifying and uncontainable.

Off-stage, Tina's style was as distinct as her music. Her fashion choices, often bold and unconventional, became emblematic of her personal and artistic independence. The mini-skirts, the high-heels, the wild hair – each aspect of her look was a statement, defining a new archetype for female artists in the music industry.

Tina's influence on music extended far beyond her own discography. Many artists, including Beyoncé and Rihanna, have cited her as an inspiration, acknowledging the path she paved for them. Her style and sound have become reference points in music history, and her spirit and resilience continue to inspire artists worldwide.

In retrospect, the impact of Tina Turner on the music industry becomes undeniable. From the young girl singing in Nutbush's choir to the global superstar selling out stadiums, Tina's journey was marked by relentless determination and unparalleled talent. Her influence is deeply etched in the fabric of music, her legacy enduring in every artist she inspired and every life she touched with her music.

As we remember Tina Turner, we celebrate not just an artist, but an icon. Her music, style, and spirit revolutionized the industry and shaped the path for those that followed. "Iconic Tina" indeed, a testament to a life that transformed music and left an indelible mark on the world.

# Moment Nr. 30

---

# The Passing of a Legend: Reflecting on Her Life and Influence Following Her Passing

May 24, 2023, marked a moment of profound grief and reflection. The iconic Tina Turner, the undisputed queen of Rock 'n' Roll, had drawn her final breath. Yet, even in her absence, her spirit lingered, the echoes of her life's symphony resonating through the lives of millions she'd touched.

Anna Mae Bullock, a little girl born in the quiet town of Nutbush, Tennessee, could never have known the extraordinary journey awaiting her. It was a journey that would see her rise from humble beginnings to worldwide acclaim. As we reflect on her birth, we're reminded of her early passion for music, her palpable talent, and the unshakeable will that propelled her into the stratosphere of legendary musicians.

The world knew her as Tina Turner, but behind the glittering stage lights and curtain calls was a testament to human resilience. Her life was marked by struggles and trials, each one an intense melody in the grand opera of her existence. Her story was a testament to the human spirit's capacity to endure, to transform, and ultimately, to soar.

In her passing, the world didn't just lose a remarkable artist; it bid farewell to a woman who personified strength and tenacity. Yet, the end of her life didn't signify the end of her influence. As mournful tunes of "Proud Mary" and "Simply the Best" echoed across radio stations and filled the hearts of grieving fans, the legacy of Tina Turner continued to inspire and uplift.

Music was Tina's gift to the world, and what a spectacular gift it was. Her distinctive voice and her raw, energetic performances revolutionized the music scene, bringing a fresh, powerful sound that remains unmatched. The impact of her unique style transcended the boundaries of her genre, leaving an indelible mark on the music industry that continues to inspire artists today.

But Tina's influence wasn't confined to the realm of music. Her life story — a tale of survival, resilience, and relentless pursuit of dreams against overwhelming odds — resonated deeply with millions. She embodied a beacon of hope and a shining example of the potential within us all to rise above our circumstances.

Remembering Tina Turner is to celebrate an extraordinary life that has left a timeless legacy. It's a celebration of a voice that enthralled, a spirit that inspired, and a heart that never lost its beat, even in the face of adversity. The narrative of her life serves as an eternal melody, a source of inspiration, and a testament to the enduring power of resilience and courage.

The dawn of Tina's life began in a small town but her sunset left a glow that encompasses the globe. Though she is no longer with us, her legacy, encapsulated in her music and her remarkable life story, lives on. It continues to empower, to inspire, and to remind us all that no matter the trials we face, we, like Tina, can remain 'simply the best'.

# PART 08: Global Superstar

# Moment Nr. 31

## *Break Every Rule: The Making of Tina's Sixth Solo Album*

As we reflect on the birth of Anna Mae Bullock and the global impact of the woman she would become – the legendary Tina Turner – it is impossible not to marvel at the pivotal moments that punctuated her illustrious career. One such moment was the creation of her sixth solo album, 'Break Every Rule', a daring venture that further solidified her status as a musical icon.

In the mid-1980s, the music industry trembled in anticipation as Tina Turner prepared to unleash her audacious new project. 'Break Every Rule' was not just an album; it was a declaration, a bold statement of intent from a woman unafraid to challenge conventions and defy expectations. Much like her life, this album was a testament to her courageous spirit, a defiance against the norms, and a relentless pursuit of her own truth.

Creating 'Break Every Rule' was an immense undertaking, the result of countless hours in the recording studio, tireless rehearsals, and an unwavering commitment to her artistic vision. Despite the high stakes and the immense pressure that came with the follow-up to her hugely successful album 'Private Dancer', Tina did not compromise. She pushed boundaries, explored new musical directions, and poured her heart and soul into every track.

The result was a masterpiece that echoed the resilience, passion, and indomitable spirit of Tina herself. 'Break Every Rule' saw Tina dancing to her own rhythm, a tapestry of genres interwoven, reflecting the eclectic blend of influences that had shaped her unique style. It was raw, emotional, and undeniably authentic.

Songs like "Typical Male" and "Two People" showcased Tina's incomparable vocal prowess and unique style. Every track felt like an intimate conversation, a glimpse into the heart and mind of a woman who had weathered storms and emerged stronger. The lyrics told stories of love, loss, resilience, and defiance, themes that resonated deeply with her audience and echoed the trials and triumphs of her own journey.


The album's global success was a testament to Tina's extraordinary talent and her ability to connect with fans across the world. It topped charts, earned platinum certifications, and sparked a world-wide concert tour, further propelling Tina into the stratosphere of musical legends.

The creation of 'Break Every Rule' was a pivotal moment in Tina Turner's career, a testament to her artistry, resilience, and unyielding determination to create music that was true to herself. It was a reflection of a remarkable woman, a woman born in a small town who had the courage to dream, the will to fight, and the talent to take the world by storm.

Today, as we remember Tina, we celebrate not only her immense musical contributions but the spirit of defiance and determination that 'Break Every Rule' embodied. In her music, as in her life, Tina Turner truly broke every rule and in doing so, became 'simply the best'.

# Moment Nr. 32

## Guinness World Record: Highlighting Her 1988 Record for the Largest Paying Audience for a Solo Performer

From her humble beginnings in Nutbush, Tennessee, to the world's grandest stages, Tina Turner's journey was nothing short of extraordinary. She was born Anna Mae Bullock on a cold November day in 1939, unbeknownst to the world that she was destined to become a legend. One defining moment in her illustrious career arrived in 1988, when she secured a place in the Guinness World Records for the largest paying audience for a solo performer.

The stage was set in Rio de Janeiro's Maracanã Stadium, a venue renowned for hosting monumental events. The energy was palpable. A sea of people stretched as far as the eye could see, a sight that even seasoned performers would find awe-inspiring. Yet, Tina was in her element. She was not just a woman with a powerful voice and electric stage presence. She was an unstoppable force, ready to make history.

As the stadium lights illuminated the night, a staggering 188,000 fans waited in anticipation. This wasn't just another concert. It was a testament to Tina Turner's undeniable appeal and her power to transcend borders, cultures, and generations. Her performance that night, a part of her "Break Every Rule World Tour", would forever etch her name into the annals of music history.

Her record-breaking concert was not just about the size of the crowd. It symbolized Tina's resilience, her ability to rise from the ashes, and her refusal to let adversity define her. It was a triumphant moment that marked the peak of her comeback, a testament to her ability to captivate audiences around the world.

The roar of the crowd when Tina stepped onto the stage was more than just adoration for a music superstar; it was a recognition of her journey. From her difficult beginnings and turbulent personal life to her transformation into a global icon, Tina Turner had fought for every bit of her success. The record-breaking audience was a testament to her immense talent and the enduring power of her music.


That moment in Rio de Janeiro is not merely a note in a record book. It is a symbol of Tina Turner's immense impact and global reach. It is a testament to a girl from a small town who dared to dream, dared to fight, and dared to become a superstar. A woman who, with her tenacity and talent, captured the hearts of millions, breaking every rule along the way to become 'simply the best.'

As we remember Tina Turner and her indelible legacy, we reflect on the sheer power of her presence and the profundity of her journey. The record she set in 1988 stands as a testament to her unparalleled impact in the music world, a momentous achievement in a life filled with them.

# Moment Nr. 33

## Foreign Affair: Insights into the Creation and Success of this European-Focused Album

Born Anna Mae Bullock on a frosty November day in 1939, Tina Turner was a phoenix who rose from the ashes of hardship to illuminate the world with her music. Her inspiring journey led her to unparalleled heights, with one of her most significant milestones being the release of her seventh solo album, "Foreign Affair."

"Foreign Affair" was more than just another notch in Tina's belt of hits; it was a testament to her musical prowess and unyielding spirit. Released in 1989, this European-focused album was the culmination of Tina's personal and professional journey, a shining symbol of her ability to channel life's trials into compelling, soul-stirring music.

The creation process of "Foreign Affair" highlighted Tina's profound connection with Europe, a continent that played a significant role in her career resurgence. It was here that Tina found the recognition she so deserved, and it was this love from her European fans that fueled the creation of this album. She collaborated with renowned British musicians and producers, further accentuating the European influence on the album.

The result was an exhilarating mix of pop, rock, and soul that captivated millions. Songs like "The Best" and "I Don't Wanna Lose

You" demonstrated the potency of her voice and the depth of her artistry. These tracks echoed with the resilience and vibrancy that defined Tina Turner, resonating with fans across the globe.

"Foreign Affair" was a massive commercial success, particularly in Europe, where it topped the charts in multiple countries. The enduring popularity of songs like "The Best," a veritable anthem of self-belief and determination, extended the reach of Tina's music, touching the lives of listeners far and wide.

But beyond its commercial success, "Foreign Affair" held a deeper significance. It symbolized Tina's enduring love affair with Europe and its people, a relationship that had a profound influence on her music and her life. It also marked a point in her career where she was not just an American star but a global phenomenon.

As we remember Tina Turner, we celebrate not just the milestones in her career, but also the incredible journey that led her to them. "Foreign Affair" is a testament to Tina's boundless talent, resilience, and the universal appeal of her music. It stands as a shining example of her ability to turn pain into power, challenges into triumphs, and experiences into timeless music.

From a small-town girl to a global superstar, Tina Turner's story is one of extraordinary resilience and indomitable spirit. As we reflect on the journey behind "Foreign Affair", we are reminded of the power of music, the strength of resilience, and the magic that happens when you never stop believing in your dreams. Tina Turner was, and always will be, 'simply the best.'

# Moment Nr. 34

## *Farewell Tour: Reflections on her 2000 Twenty-Four Seven Tour*

In the heartland of Tennessee, on November 26, 1939, a voice was born to the world. This voice, belonging to Anna Mae Bullock, better known as Tina Turner, would rise to echo across continents and transcend time itself. A significant moment in her illustrious career, Tina's farewell tour, the "Twenty-Four Seven Tour" in 2000, embodies her resilience, power, and indomitable spirit.

Tina was not just an artist but a force of nature. Her performances were not merely concerts, but electrifying celebrations of life and music. The "Twenty-Four Seven Tour" was an epitome of this. As the millennium dawned, Tina, then 60, embarked on what she announced as her final world tour. It was her grand farewell, a culmination of a musical journey that spanned over four decades.

The tour was a testament to Tina's boundless energy and unmatched stage presence. From Los Angeles to London, she delivered performances that were as fiery and passionate as ever. Age did not dim her spirit, nor did it mute her voice. Instead, it added an element of wisdom and grace to her performances, a sense of a life well-lived and a journey well-traveled.

A highlight of the "Twenty-Four Seven Tour" was her performance at Wembley Stadium in London, where Tina held the audience captive with her electrifying charisma and soul-stirring vocals. Her rendition of songs like "Simply the Best" and "Proud Mary" left the audience in awe. Here was a woman who had faced numerous hardships and yet stood tall, her spirit unbroken, her voice undiminished.

The "Twenty-Four Seven Tour" was a commercial success, becoming the highest-grossing tour of 2000. But its significance went beyond numbers. It represented a moment of triumph for Tina, a symbol of her resilience and enduring appeal. Even as she bid adieu to the stage, she remained a beacon of inspiration, a testament to the power of perseverance.

Reflecting on Tina's farewell tour, we see a woman who has given her all to her craft. A woman who broke barriers and defied conventions to leave an indelible mark on the world of music. A woman who embraced life with all its challenges and turned her trials into triumphs.

From the humble beginnings in Nutbush, Tennessee, to her farewell tour as a global superstar, Tina Turner's journey is a story of resilience, courage, and unyielding determination. It is a narrative that tells us that no matter where we come from or what adversities we face, we have within us the power to rise and shine.

As we remember Tina Turner, we celebrate not just her career milestones, but the spirit that powered her extraordinary journey. The "Twenty-Four Seven Tour" was not a goodbye, but a 'thank you' from Tina to her fans worldwide. It was a tribute to a lifetime of music, resilience, and most importantly, a love affair with life itself. After all, in the words of Tina herself, "Life is a party. Dress for it."

# Moment Nr. 35

## *All the Best: The Story behind her 2004 Compilation Album*

From the rural landscapes of Tennessee emerged a powerful voice, a voice that would, in time, rise above the ordinary, break the barriers, and touch millions of hearts around the globe. This voice belonged to Anna Mae Bullock, the world knows better as Tina Turner. On this remarkable journey, a standout moment was the release of her 2004 compilation album, "All the Best."

By 2004, Tina Turner had established herself as a monumental figure in the music industry. Her music - a melodic amalgamation of rock, soul, and pop - had etched itself in the hearts of listeners worldwide. The compilation album, "All the Best," was a hand-picked selection of her works, a musical treat and a heartfelt tribute to her fans.

The album was a journey across time and sound, showcasing her versatility as an artist. From her iconic hits such as "What's Love Got to Do with It" and "Proud Mary," to her soul-stirring renditions of "Private Dancer" and "River Deep – Mountain High," every track on the album was a testament to her vocal prowess and her ability to connect with her audience.

"All The Best" was not just an album; it was a musical odyssey that captured the essence of Tina Turner. It encapsulated her triumphs and her trials, her resilience and her determination. Listening to it was like walking alongside Tina on her journey, from Nutbush to global stardom.

But the album was more than just a collection of songs; it was a celebration of Tina's journey, her victories, her life. The track "Open Arms," a poignant ballad about embracing love and life, resonated deeply with the listeners, encapsulating Tina's spirit.

"All The Best" was received with widespread acclaim and commercial success. It became a multi-platinum record, underscoring the enduring appeal of Tina's music. More than two decades into her solo career, she was still touching hearts, still resonating with listeners old and new.

In retrospect, the title "All the Best" was apt, for it represented the best of Tina Turner. It showcased her growth as an artist, her evolution as a performer, and her indomitable spirit. It was an embodiment of her belief in love, resilience, and the power of music.

Looking back on Tina Turner's life and career, one can't help but admire her tenacity and strength. Born in a small town, she overcame numerous obstacles to reach the pinnacle of global stardom. The release of "All the Best" was not just a milestone in her career, but also a testament to her resilience and passion.

Tina Turner was more than just a global music sensation; she was a woman of strength, a beacon of resilience, a symbol of triumph. Her music is her legacy, a legacy that continues to inspire and empower. As we remember Tina, we don't just celebrate her music, we celebrate her spirit, her determination, her undying belief in herself. "All The Best" is not just an album, it is a tribute to this extraordinary woman. It is a testament to a life that was, indeed, simply the best.

# PART 09: A Resilient Spirit

# Moment Nr. 36

## *Health Struggles: An intimate look into Tina's battle with illness*

There is a profound beauty in resilience, an irresistible allure in the strength of a spirit that refuses to break, no matter the weight it bears. This resilience, this fierce determination, was the beating heart of Tina Turner's extraordinary journey. This facet of her life shone through in her battles, not just against the trials of stardom, but the personal wars waged within the confines of her own body.

Tina's health struggles were not publicly known for a significant portion of her life, hidden beneath the glow of her electrifying performances and iconic voice. But behind the dazzling spectacle of her life as a global superstar, Tina was facing an intimately personal struggle.

Her health issues began with high blood pressure, leading to a stroke after her farewell tour in 2009. The strength that saw her through a tumultuous personal life and an exhaustive career again came to the fore. True to her nature, she took on the challenge head-on, battling through rehabilitation, and by her account, was walking again in just three weeks.

Her health, however, would throw another curveball. In 2016, Tina was diagnosed with intestinal cancer. But even in the face of this life-threatening disease, Tina's spirit remained unbroken. Opting for homeopathic remedies over chemotherapy, she showcased a bold approach to her health, an approach that echoed the defiance she demonstrated throughout her life.

In a twist of fate, her body started rejecting the treatment, leading to kidney failure. But, as the saying goes, when one door closes, another opens. Erwin Bach, her long-time partner, and husband offered one of his kidneys. Their love story, filled with mutual respect and admiration, was further solidified by this act of supreme love and sacrifice.

Tina's health journey was not merely a story of struggles; it was a testament to the undying human spirit, the will to survive, and the strength to face adversity. It's about a woman whose courage resonated as profoundly off-stage as her voice did on-stage. The pain and the trials never defined her; instead, they highlighted her perseverance, adding another facet to the multi-dimensional figure we admire as Tina Turner.

In looking at Tina's battle with illness, we see the human behind the superstar—the woman who, despite the glamour and fame, faced deeply personal struggles that many of us can relate to. We see a woman who, even in her darkest hours, held fast to hope and resilience, embodying the power of the human spirit to overcome.

Her journey serves as a testament to the strength that lies within us all, a beacon of hope for anyone battling their personal storms. It is a message of resilience, a story of survival. This is the spirit of Tina Turner, a spirit that was, and forever will be, simply the best.

# Moment Nr. 37

## *The Gift of Life: The Emotional Journey of her Kidney transplant, with her husband, Erwin, as the Donor*

Within every heartbeat of Tina Turner's life resided an unquenchable spirit of survival, a force that powered her through the tumultuous storms of her journey. This spirit shone its brightest when her health issues escalated to the brink of life itself.

By 2016, Tina faced one of her most formidable challenges yet - intestinal cancer. After a brave battle, she opted for homeopathic remedies over chemotherapy. However, fate had a different path for Tina. Her body began rejecting the treatment, leading to kidney failure. The woman, who had fought her way to the top of the music industry and survived the torments of her personal life, was now wrestling with her own body in a struggle for survival.

Enter Erwin Bach, Tina's husband, her rock, her confidant, her soulmate. In an act of love and selflessness that few can fathom, he offered her a lifeline - one of his kidneys. Love stories are often painted in romantic hues and grand gestures, but here was an act of love that was life itself, a gift not of roses or diamonds, but of time, of life, of a future.

The emotional journey of the kidney transplant was a complex tapestry woven with threads of fear, anxiety, hope, and unparalleled love. The couple faced the uncertainty and risks of the procedure, their resilience and their bond becoming their most potent weapon. This chapter of Tina's life, while fraught with hardship and the shadow of mortality, highlighted the extraordinary depth of her relationship with Erwin, a relationship built on a foundation of mutual respect, admiration, and profound love.

Tina, always the fighter, emerged from the transplant with a new lease on life. The journey had been treacherous, the emotional turmoil immense, but the woman who had once belted out, "What's love got to do with it?" found herself in the embrace of a love that had everything to do with it. It was love that saw her through, love that gave her the strength to fight, love that bestowed upon her the gift of life.

This tale of survival and profound love adds a rich layer to the legacy of Tina Turner. It underscores not only the resilience that was a hallmark of her character but the depths of her human experience. It paints a picture of a woman who, even in the face of death, was a testament to the strength and power of the human spirit, buoyed by a love that transcended the ordinary.

In remembering Tina Turner, we remember this resilience, this spirit, this love. We celebrate a life that impacted millions, a life that sang the anthem of survival, a life that, till its final note, was indeed, simply the best.

# Moment Nr. 38

## Moving Beyond Music: Exploration of Tina's ventures outside of music, such as her Involvement in the Fashion World

Born into a humble household in Nutbush, Tennessee, little did Anna Mae Bullock know that she was destined to be the legendary Tina Turner, a name that would resonate with millions worldwide. From this humble beginning, Tina rose to international stardom, her music becoming the lifeblood of an era. However, her creative genius was not bound by the realm of music alone. Tina's indomitable spirit and unique sense of style led her to make a mark in another arena - the fashion world.

Tina Turner was not merely a follower of fashion; she was a trend-setter. Her fiery presence on stage was magnified by her bold, distinctive style - a blend of glitz, glamour, and rock and roll. Her daring fashion choices were as much a part of her persona as her powerful voice. Turner's fashion statement was a vivid reflection of her strength, her energy, and her audacity.

Beyond the stage, her keen interest in fashion led her to collaborate with top fashion designers like Giorgio Armani, who was behind her extravagant concert costumes. Such alliances allowed her to imbue the world of fashion with her unique aesthetic, influencing a generation of fashionistas and designers alike.

Tina's ventures into the world of fashion were not merely commercial endeavors; they were an extension of her creative expression. Her iconic look, characterized by high-heels, miniskirts, and her wild, lioness-like hair, transcended the norm, just as her music had. Tina Turner, the fashion icon, was born.

This exploration into fashion was also reflective of Tina's philosophy of life – to break boundaries and explore the uncharted. Here was a woman who was unafraid of reinventing herself, of stepping out of her comfort zone. From music to fashion, her life was a symphony of bold moves and innovative choices.

As we delve into this chapter of Tina's life, we witness a woman who was not just a music sensation but a global icon, influencing various spheres of art and culture. This journey into the fashion world reflects her multifaceted persona, the many hues that made up the vibrant tapestry of Tina Turner's life.

In remembering Tina Turner, we remember not just the music legend, but the trendsetter, the fashion icon, the woman who dared to venture beyond her established domain and make her mark in another. We celebrate the spirit that dared to dream, dared to explore, dared to be different.

Tina Turner's legacy is not confined to the songs she sang but extends to the lives she touched and the norms she challenged. Her journey from a small-town girl to a global icon is an ode to resilience, courage, and the spirit of exploration. This, in her own words, was her way of living life "simply the best."

# PART 10: Deepening Her Legacy

# Moment Nr. 39

## *Rock and Roll Hall of Fame: Her Induction and what it Signifies in her Career*

There are moments in a musician's life that solidify their standing in the annals of music history, one such moment for Tina Turner came on a remarkable day when she was inducted into the prestigious Rock and Roll Hall of Fame. This pivotal event was not just a crowning achievement of her career, but a testament to the seismic impact she had made on the world of music.

Born Anna Mae Bullock in a small town called Nutbush, Tennessee, Tina began her journey singing in her local church choir. From these humble beginnings, she rose to heights many only dream of, becoming a global music sensation revered by countless fans and fellow artists.

Tina Turner's induction into the Rock and Roll Hall of Fame came in 1991. It was a glorious moment that encapsulated the hard work, talent, and resilience that characterized her astounding career. The ceremony was not just about honoring her contribution to music; it was a testament to her strength and determination, qualities that propelled her through various challenges and obstacles she faced throughout her life.

The Rock and Roll Hall of Fame is not simply a museum; it's a pantheon of the greatest contributors to the genre. To be inducted is to be recognized as a defining force, an individual who has shaped the course of rock and roll. When Tina Turner was ushered into this exclusive club, it was an acknowledgment that she was not just a participant, but a pathfinder in the world of music.

The strength of Turner's legacy lies not only in her music but also in the sheer force of her personality. Her fiery performances, her distinctively raspy voice, and her incredible resilience in the face of adversity have left a lasting impact on rock and roll. Her induction into the Hall of Fame was a nod to these exceptional qualities and her enduring influence on music.


Remembering Tina Turner is to remember a woman who refused to be confined by expectations, who shattered barriers and crafted a legacy marked by tenacity, talent, and triumph. She was a woman born to humble beginnings, who went on to command the world's stage, and whose music still echoes in the hearts of millions.

Her induction into the Rock and Roll Hall of Fame was a defining moment, a time when the world stood in unanimous agreement, honoring a woman who had inspired and entertained us all. It signified the deepening of her legacy, one that transcends music and serves as a beacon of courage and resilience.

In celebrating Tina Turner, we don't merely celebrate a gifted musician, but a remarkable woman whose spirit echoed in every note she sang. The story of Tina Turner is a testament to the transformative power of music, and her induction into the Hall of Fame is a significant chapter in this extraordinary tale. It serves as a reminder that she was, indeed, simply the best.

# Moment Nr. 40

## *Beyond: Tina's Involvement in this Spiritual Music Project*

While Tina Turner's towering musical legacy is known to all, an equally powerful, albeit lesser-known facet of her journey, is her deep spiritual exploration. Her involvement with the 'Beyond' project is a testament to this pursuit. This endeavor was not just a detour from her iconic rock persona, but a profound expression of the spiritual dimension that came to shape her life and artistry.

Born in Nutbush, Tennessee, Tina Turner, christened Anna Mae Bullock, embarked on a journey that would take her from the cotton fields of her childhood to the zenith of the music world. Amidst her rise to stardom and the trials she faced, Turner found solace in spirituality, which became a critical aspect of her personal and professional journey. The 'Beyond' project was a testament to this intimate side of her life.

The 'Beyond' project was a musical exploration of faith and spirituality. Tina, along with Regula Curti and Dechen Shak-Dagsay, created music that transcended religious boundaries and brought to the forefront the universal values of love, peace, and unity. For Turner, it was a means to communicate her spiritual journey and share the transformative power of spirituality with her global audience.

Turner's involvement in the 'Beyond' project was not a sudden departure but a natural progression. Her exploration of Buddhism in the mid-70s provided her with the strength and resilience to navigate through the turbulent times of her life. The project allowed her to express the spiritual resilience that defined her personal journey, and through her mesmerizing voice, she invited others to experience the same solace and strength.

Her work in 'Beyond' is a testament to her belief that music is a universal language, one that transcends boundaries, be they geographical or religious. The project sought to harness this power to spread the message of love, unity, and inner peace.


In the 'Beyond' project, Tina Turner ventured beyond the realms of pop and rock, beyond fame and material success. She moved towards a universal spiritual message, demonstrating a resilience that stood not just on stages, but also in the face of life's most profound questions.

Remembering Tina Turner means remembering not just a global music sensation, but a woman whose spirit remained undefeated in the face of adversity, a woman whose faith shaped her life as much as her music. Her journey is a testament to the indomitable spirit that can rise from a small town in Tennessee to touch millions of hearts worldwide, not just through music, but through a shared quest for inner peace and unity.

Her involvement in 'Beyond' was not a footnote in her illustrious career, but a significant chapter in the story of a woman who dared to move beyond expectations, beyond hardships, beyond even music, to explore a world steeped in spirituality. It underlines the fact that while she was a music icon, she was also a woman whose faith and spirit truly made her 'simply the best.'

# Moment Nr. 41

## *Her Swiss Citizenship: Details about her decision to adopt Swiss citizenship.*

In 2013, Tina Turner's illustrious career had spanned over half a century, transforming her from a girl born in the small town of Nutbush, Tennessee, into a global music sensation. But as her music resonated across continents, she was quietly cultivating another, more personal transformation: her journey towards Swiss citizenship.

Tina's connection to Switzerland began in 1994 when she settled into a picturesque home by Lake Zurich with her long-term partner, German music executive Erwin Bach. Over the years, she fell in love with the tranquil landscapes, the sense of security, and the overall quality of life that Switzerland offered. In an interview, she expressed how living there felt like "home", a sanctuary away from the media frenzy that had often surrounded her life.

The decision to pursue Swiss citizenship, announced in 2013, may have seemed surprising to the world outside, but for Tina, it was a natural progression of her life's journey. Just as she had done in her music, Tina chose a path of authenticity and heartfelt connection. Embracing Switzerland as her home was more than a legal formality; it was a testament to her ability to redefine herself, to create her own sense of belonging.

In becoming a Swiss citizen, Tina Turner was also embracing a deeper commitment to her adopted home. She studied the Swiss German dialect, history, and the local political structure, demonstrating a profound respect for her new homeland. These efforts weren't just about fulfilling legal requirements—they symbolized her dedication to fully engage with the life she had chosen.

Tina Turner's decision to adopt Swiss citizenship was a milestone that expanded the global dimensions of her life, weaving her story more deeply into the tapestry of the international community. In this moment, as in so many others, Tina Turner was not just a music icon, but a global citizen. She had an ability to transcend boundaries, not only in music, but also in her personal life. Her journey serves as a beacon, illuminating the possibility of change, growth, and finding home in unexpected places.

Tina Turner's Swiss citizenship isn't just a detail in her biography. It's a chapter in her life that encapsulates a message she conveyed throughout her career and personal life: resilience, transformation, and above all, a relentless pursuit of happiness. Her decision to become a Swiss citizen was Simply The Best choice for her, a testament to the life she led, and a legacy that continues to inspire millions around the world. In her music and her life, Tina Turner demonstrated that we can indeed, with courage and determination, navigate our own unique paths.

Just as she sang, Tina Turner taught us how to keep on rollin', whether on a river or amidst the serene beauty of Switzerland. Her legacy continues to resonate globally, reminding us all of the extraordinary power of authenticity, resilience, and personal transformation.

# Moment Nr. 42

## *The Tina Turner Musical: An Inside Look into the Creation and Success of this Stage Musical*

It was a life story written in power chords and soaring vocals, punctuated with trials, victories, heartaches, and triumphs. It was a tale that echoed from the humble cotton fields of Nutbush, Tennessee, and roared across the most prestigious stages worldwide. The story of Tina Turner, one that would inspire and uplift millions, was a natural fit for the world of musical theatre. With the creation and success of "Tina: The Tina Turner Musical," Tina's life was immortalized not just in the annals of music history, but in the vibrant world of Broadway.

When "Tina: The Tina Turner Musical" first opened its doors, the audience was presented with a story that transcended the typical rock biography. Instead, they were invited to witness an intimate journey that celebrated the woman behind the legendary persona. It was a testament to the unwavering resilience and sheer talent that propelled Anna Mae Bullock from a small-town girl to a global music icon.

The creation of the musical was a labor of love, drawn from years of interviews, personal testimonies, and with the invaluable input of Tina herself. Every note sung, every word spoken, was imbued with the authenticity of a life lived in full color and resounding tenacity.

The show masterfully encapsulated Tina's magnetic energy, indomitable spirit, and infectious zest for life. It resonated with the compelling narrative of her rise to stardom, her struggles, and her eventual triumphant emergence as the undisputed queen of rock 'n' roll.

The success of the musical can be attributed to its authenticity. It did not shy away from the darker chapters of her life, but instead, showcased how these trials only amplified her strength and resilience. It was an homage to a woman who did not just survive but thrived, changing the face of music in the process.

"Tina: The Tina Turner Musical" was also a celebration of her immense talent. It reminded the world of her electrifying performances, her gritty, soulful voice, and her incredible ability to captivate audiences. The stage came alive with renditions of her hits, filling the theater with the same vibrant energy that she exuded in her live performances.

The legacy of Tina Turner is a beacon of resilience and inspiration. The musical adaptation of her life carries forward this legacy, touching new generations with her empowering story. It stands as a testament to a woman who, in overcoming her struggles, became an emblem of courage and determination.

To know Tina Turner is to understand that she was more than a phenomenal singer; she was a woman of unyielding spirit. Her story, so beautifully captured in "Tina: The Tina Turner Musical," is a testament to her incredible journey – a journey that started in the unassuming town of Nutbush and, against all odds, led her to global stardom. A journey that proves, indeed, she is 'simply the best.'

# Moment Nr. 43

## *Happiness Becomes You: A Discussion of Tina's guide to Happiness, infused with her Buddhist beliefs*

Tina Turner's life was a symphony of resilience, punctuated by high notes of triumph and low notes of adversity. Through every twist and turn, she remained steadfast, forging an indelible path of perseverance. This enduring spirit was crystallized in her book, "Happiness Becomes You: A Journey of Trials to Triumph," a reflection of her Buddhist beliefs and a testament to her journey towards inner peace and happiness.

Born into hardship in Nutbush, Tennessee, Tina's early life was filled with adversity. From her tumultuous relationship with Ike Turner to her courageous departure and subsequent rise to global stardom, Tina's life had been a testament to endurance and grit. But amidst the whirlwind of her external life, Tina embarked on an internal journey, seeking a spiritual solace that would ultimately transform her.

In the early 1970s, Tina was introduced to Nichiren Buddhism. The teachings resonated with her, offering a sanctuary of tranquility amidst her turbulent life. The faith taught her to manifest happiness not as an external pursuit, but as an internal state of being, an evolution that can be cultivated through mindful actions and a steadfast spirit.

"Happiness Becomes You" is more than just a guide to joy; it is a deeply personal exploration of Tina's spiritual journey. It is an honest and heartfelt discourse that offers a window into her soul, revealing the spiritual tenets that allowed her to navigate life's stormiest waters with grace and unwavering optimism.

The book is filled with the echoes of her powerful voice, resonating with wisdom, compassion, and unwavering hope. Tina's guide to happiness is infused with her unwavering belief in the power of the human spirit, the tenacity of the will, and the transformational magic of faith.


Through her Buddhist beliefs, Tina found a way to transmute suffering into growth, pain into power, and adversity into victory. She credits her spiritual journey as the pivotal shift that allowed her to thrive amidst trials, to find happiness amidst heartache, and ultimately, to become the woman that millions admire today.

The strength of "Happiness Becomes You" lies in its universal appeal. It encapsulates the human experience, touching upon shared struggles, dreams, and the innate desire for happiness. Yet, it remains unmistakably Tina, a testament to her unique journey, her unwavering spirit, and her boundless capacity to inspire.

In "Happiness Becomes You," Tina Turner's voice echoes with the same power and passion that has defined her legendary career. Yet, instead of singing a song, she is imparting wisdom, sharing a piece of her soul, and inviting readers to embrace the beauty of life's journey.

Through this spiritual guide, Tina Turner continues to inspire, just as she did with her music. She celebrates the power of resilience, offers a testament to the transformative power of faith, and invites us all to understand that indeed, happiness can become us.

# Moment Nr. 44

## *The Tina Turner Documentary: Insights into the making and the release of this HBO documentary.*

In 2021, Tina Turner's life and career found a new, immersive platform through the documentary simply titled "Tina," released by HBO. This intimate and heartfelt portrait of the queen of rock 'n' roll was a resounding testament to her strength, resilience, and the enduring power of her music.

The creation of the documentary was a collaboration between directors Daniel Lindsay and T.J. Martin, both of whom were deeply committed to presenting an authentic narrative of Tina's life. They delved into the private and public aspects of her existence, showcasing not just the performer, but also the person behind the music.

"Tina" was crafted with meticulous attention to detail. It combined rare archival footage, audio tapes, personal photos, and new interviews, to present a compelling narrative. With Tina's direct involvement, the documentary gave audiences a unique window into her life, her struggles, and her triumphs. It was a chance to see the woman behind the legend, and to understand her journey through her own words.

One of the most impactful aspects of "Tina" was its unflinching depiction of the hardships Tina faced. It dealt with her abusive relationship with Ike Turner, her financial struggles, and her monumental comeback. This raw honesty was an essential component of the documentary, providing viewers a glimpse into Tina's resilience and tenacity, and an understanding of how she managed to rise above these challenges.

But "Tina" was not just a story of survival. It was also a celebration. It showcased her meteoric rise to fame in the 1980s, her iconic performances, and her lasting impact on the music industry. The documentary captured the incredible energy of her performances, her commanding stage presence, and her unparalleled vocal talent.

When "Tina" was released in 2021, it was met with critical acclaim and viewer admiration worldwide. It solidified Tina's status as an enduring icon, reminding us of her indomitable spirit and extraordinary talent.

Tina Turner's participation in the documentary represented her unwavering commitment to truth. She courageously shared her story, even the painful parts, to remind everyone that it's possible to overcome adversity and achieve greatness.

In this subchapter of her legacy, the HBO documentary "Tina" stands as a testament to the power of authenticity and courage. It encapsulates a pivotal moment in Tina Turner's career, a moment where she stepped back onto the stage not just as a performer, but as a narrator of her own life story. She offered the world a raw, honest, and inspiring glimpse into her journey from a small-town girl to a global sensation, teaching us all the true meaning of resilience, determination, and the power of staying "Simply The Best."

# PART II: The Final Years

# Moment Nr. 45

## *Life in Retirement: An Exploration of Tina's Life away from the Stage*

The grandeur of Tina Turner's legacy was not confined to her time beneath the stage lights, nor did it diminish with her decision to step away from them. The stage may have been her platform, but the woman we celebrate today was born long before the first note was sung, before the spotlight first found her. This woman, born Anna Mae Bullock on a fateful day in Nutbush, Tennessee, would always be more than just 'Tina Turner' the icon. She was, and always will be, simply the best - in music, in resilience, and in life.

When Tina decided to retire, she didn't fade into the background. Instead, she embarked on a quieter but no less extraordinary journey. In retirement, she found a life rich in experiences, brimming with love and contentment. After decades of taking the world by storm, she embraced the tranquility and freedom her new life offered, illuminating the path of her life with a different kind of spotlight.

Tina chose to retire in Switzerland, a land renowned for its picturesque landscapes and peaceful serenity. She exchanged the dazzling stage lights for the gentle, golden glow of Swiss sunsets, the thrumming basslines for the tranquil sounds of Lake Zurich. It was in this idyllic setting that Tina found a different kind of stage, one that celebrated the quiet beauty of life's simple pleasures.

Her home, a sprawling Chateau aptly named the "Chateau Algonquin," was a testament to her refined taste. More than just a stunning piece of architecture, it was a sanctuary, an oasis away from the public eye. She cherished her privacy, savoring moments of solitude and tranquility, a stark contrast to her vibrant life on stage.

But even in retirement, Tina never stopped being the powerhouse that she was. She continued to engage with her passions, whether it was working on her book, "Happiness Becomes You," or participating in the creation of "TINA: The Tina Turner Musical." The fervor that fueled her music career found new avenues of expression, marking her retirement years with a different, but no less significant, form of accomplishment.

Tina's retired life was richly adorned with love. Her marriage to Erwin Bach, her partner of over 30 years, was a beacon of her personal life. Their bond, steadfast and unwavering, was the bedrock upon which Tina built her life in retirement. They found joy in the simplicity of their shared life, in quiet moments by Lake Zurich, in their shared love for gardening and their shared appreciation for the arts.

Tina Turner's retirement was not a conclusion, but a continuation. She simply traded one stage for another, exchanging the glamour and applause of her music career for the quiet beauty and heartfelt contentment of a private life. As we remember her, we must remember all of her - the star who enthralled millions, and the woman who found joy in the simplicity of a life lived away from the spotlight. For it is in this dichotomy, in this holistic portrait of Tina Turner, that we truly celebrate her life. A life that was, in every sense, simply the best.

# Moment Nr. 46

## *Love Letters to Her Fans: The Impact and Importance of Tina's heartfelt letters to her fans*

There was a mutual adoration between Tina Turner and her fans, a love that ran as deep as the currents of the Mississippi River, near where she was born as Anna Mae Bullock. It was a bond forged in the heat of countless performances, nurtured over a lifetime of shared experiences. And it was during her final years that Tina found a profound way to express this love – through heartfelt letters to her fans.

Tina was aware of her influence. She knew that each lyric she sang, each beat she danced to, vibrated in the hearts of her followers. Her voice echoed in their souls, providing strength, comfort, and joy. Her gratitude towards her fans was enormous, and she sought to reciprocate the love they showered upon her, writing letters that offered a glimpse into her soul. These were not just casual notes; they were confessions of love, packed with sincerity, gratitude, and wisdom.

Tina's letters were vibrant and warm, mirroring her indomitable spirit. Each word she penned was a testament to her enduring grace, a tribute to her undying connection with her fans. She shared snippets of her life, nuggets of wisdom, and words of encouragement. They were the musings of a woman who had seen the best and worst of life, yet stood tall, unwavering, always pushing forward.

She spoke of her life experiences, drawing lessons from her journey. Tina penned down her philosophies, her beliefs, her struggles, and her victories. Through her words, she sought to empower her fans, to imbue them with the same resilience and tenacity that had fueled her remarkable journey. In her letters, Tina also candidly expressed her gratitude. She acknowledged the love of her fans, appreciating their unwavering support that had carried her through the roughest storms.

These letters were an extension of Tina herself, a pure expression of her authenticity. They bridged the gap between the iconic superstar and the individual fans, offering a personal, heartfelt connection. Her fans cherished these letters, holding onto every word as a sacred artifact from the woman they so revered.

Tina's final years were enriched by these exchanges with her fans. These letters offered her an avenue to express her appreciation, to reciprocate the love she had received throughout her career. Each letter she penned reflected the remarkable woman she was – resilient, grateful, and always loving.

On this significant day, we remember Tina Turner, a woman whose impact transcended music, whose legacy went beyond the stage. We celebrate the birth of an extraordinary woman, whose voice echoed in songs and in her love letters to her fans. These letters are more than mere words; they are a testament to the bond she shared with her fans, a manifestation of the love and respect she had for them. In celebrating Tina, we celebrate this love, this connection that continues to inspire millions around the world. And through her words, through her music, her legacy endures, a testament to a life well-lived, a life that was, truly, simply the best.

# Moment Nr. 47

## *Celebrating 80: A Reflection on her 80th birthday and how she marked this Milestone*

When Tina Turner turned 80, she had already journeyed through eight decades of life, music, resilience, and transformation. From the girl born in Nutbush, Tennessee, to a music icon known and revered worldwide, Tina's life was a testament to endurance, vitality, and the power of reinvention.

Her 80th birthday was not merely a passage of time; it was a celebration of the life and legacy of Tina Turner, a woman whose essence was as fiery and dynamic at 80 as it was at 20. This milestone was marked with jubilance and gratitude, reflection and forward-thinking, embodying the spirit that defined Tina's remarkable journey.

To celebrate her 80th birthday, Tina released a special video message for her fans worldwide. It was a heartfelt thank you, an acknowledgement of the support that had fueled her extraordinary career. In her words, "I'm 80. What did I think? How did I think I would be at 80? Not like this. How is this? I look great. I feel good. I have gone through some very serious sicknesses that I am overcoming. So, it's like having a second chance at life."

And this was Tina's essence – always acknowledging the storms she weathered, yet remaining fiercely optimistic and resilient. Her birthday was not merely a celebration of the years passed; it was an affirmation of her unwavering spirit and the continued strength she drew from her experiences.

Tina's 80th birthday was an echo of the chapters that had made up her life - each struggle faced, each victory won, each note sung. It was a tribute to her relentless spirit, her unyielding resilience, and her relentless pursuit of happiness.

The world rejoiced with Tina on her 80th birthday. From fans to fellow artists, people globally acknowledged the woman who had not just shaped music history but had also become a symbol of strength and resilience. Social media platforms buzzed with birthday wishes and tributes, each message a testament to the love and admiration held for her.

As we remember Tina Turner, we celebrate her life marked by courage and change. We remember the young girl who began singing in church choirs, the woman who rose to fame alongside Ike Turner, the solo artist who rocked the world with her fiery performances, and the woman who, even at 80, continued to inspire millions. Her 80th birthday was not merely a day on a calendar; it was a milestone that encapsulated the essence of her journey. It was a symbol of the strength and vitality that defined Tina, a testament to her ability to weather life's storms, and a celebration of her unwavering spirit. Her 80th birthday was a celebration of Tina Turner – a woman who truly was, and will always be, 'simply the best'.

# Moment Nr. 48

## *COVID-19 Pandemic: How She Navigated the Global Crisis*

As the COVID-19 pandemic swept across the globe in 2020, people of all walks of life were thrust into uncharted territories of uncertainty and isolation. However, Tina Turner—unyielding and resilient as ever—navigated these turbulent times with grace, empathy, and wisdom, embodying the essence of her lifetime mantra: the power of resilience.

At the outset of the pandemic, Tina was residing in her beautiful chateau on the banks of Lake Zurich. Her days were often spent soaking in the tranquility of her home, a far cry from the electrifying concert stages she once dominated. Despite the confinement imposed by the pandemic, Tina continued to radiate positivity, showing the world that strength and serenity could coexist even amidst chaos.

Though her private life remained largely away from public scrutiny during this time, Tina used her immense influence to inspire hope and resilience. Through sporadic online interviews and social media posts, she reached out to her fans, sharing words of comfort and courage.

She drew parallels between the ongoing crisis and her personal struggles, underscoring the power of perseverance. In one of her interviews, Tina equated the pandemic to "a hard life turning around," urging her followers to hold on to hope and affirming that the trying times would pass, just as they had in her life.

Furthermore, she found solace and strength in her longstanding practice of Buddhism. A devout follower for over four decades, Tina's faith provided her with a spiritual anchor. She shared her meditative chants with her fans online, hoping to infuse their lives with a sense of calm and resilience. It was a testament to her unwavering belief in the power of love and compassion, even in the face of overwhelming adversity.

In the face of the pandemic, Tina also showcased her generous spirit. While keeping a low profile, she supported various COVID-19 relief efforts, demonstrating her enduring commitment to humanitarian causes.

Tina Turner's navigation of the global crisis was reflective of her character: undeterred, empathetic, and perpetually hopeful. In the face of a world in turmoil, she held fast to her principles, turning inwards for strength and outwards for compassion, while championing resilience and hope. She served as a beacon of light to her millions of fans worldwide, providing them with much-needed comfort during these challenging times.

While the COVID-19 pandemic marked a dark period in global history, it also highlighted Tina's enduring spirit and her ability to inspire hope. Through her actions, she reinforced a message that had been an integral part of her life and career: that no matter the obstacles, with courage and determination, we can continue to roll on, just like the river she famously sang about.

# Moment Nr. 49

## *Her Final Public Appearance: Details of Tina's Last Public Event*

The sun had set on many days and decades since Anna Mae Bullock, a small-town girl from Nutbush, Tennessee, had transformed into Tina Turner, the queen of rock 'n' roll. The transformation was not just in name, but in spirit, strength, and artistry. From the small stages of St. Louis to the grand arenas of the world, Tina had enchanted audiences with her electrifying performances.

As we turn the pages of her illustrious life, we reach an emotional milestone—Tina's final public appearance. It took place in 2022 at the opening of 'Tina: The Tina Turner Musical,' a Broadway production in New York. Here, Tina, a living legend, was able to see her incredible journey come alive on stage, the story of a woman who had won countless battles, both on and off the stage, presented to an audience who loved and admired her.

At the grand age of 82, Tina stepped into the spotlight for the last time, gracing the audience with her radiant presence. Despite having been away from the stage for years, she exuded the same energy and passion that had characterized her iconic career. Her bright smile and indomitable spirit were undiminished, a testament to her unwavering courage and relentless optimism.

She did not perform that night, but her presence was a performance in itself, captivating and inspiring. In a touching speech, she expressed gratitude to her fans and the cast of the musical, reflecting on her life and career with grace and humility. She conveyed her joy at having her story told, highlighting the importance of resilience, determination, and self-belief.

The applause that followed was thunderous, echoing the love and admiration the audience held for her. As she waved and blew kisses to the cheering crowd, it was clear that the bond she had created with her fans was unbreakable, her impact on their lives profound.

Her final public appearance was a reflection of her life and career: powerful, inspiring, and marked by a spirit that never surrendered. It encapsulated her journey, from the fiery young artist who had revolutionized the music industry to the revered icon she had become. A woman who, in her own words, had done it "rough, tough, long, hard, and in a good way."

On May 24, 2023, just a year after this public appearance, Tina Turner passed away, leaving behind a legacy that will forever echo in the annals of music history. As we remember her life, we celebrate a woman whose strength, talent, and spirit were as electrifying as her performances. Her final public appearance, like her life, serves as an enduring reminder of her mantra: to never give up and always be 'Simply the Best'.

# Moment Nr. 50

## *Her Passing: Reflections on the Day of Her Passing and Immediate Global Reactions*

On May 24, 2023, as the world was enveloped in the ordinary humdrum of life, news began to trickle in that stilled hearts across the globe: Tina Turner, the indomitable queen of rock 'n' roll, had passed away. The air grew thick with sadness, the loss echoing far beyond the confines of her home in Zurich, reverberating in every corner of the world where her music had been a source of joy, strength, and inspiration.

Born Anna Mae Bullock, on November 26, 1939, in Nutbush, Tennessee, she had lived a life that was anything but ordinary. Her journey from a humble upbringing to the pinnacle of musical stardom was nothing short of miraculous, a testament to her unyielding spirit and unfathomable talent.

Tina's passing was not just the end of a life; it was the end of an era, a chapter in music history that was vibrant with her energy and colored by her extraordinary journey. The immediate reactions to her death bore testimony to her transcendent influence. From everyday fans to fellow artists, from local radio stations to international news agencies—every voice seemed to unite in a chorus of mourning, remembrance, and immense respect.

Social media platforms bristled with tributes as fans posted images of albums, concert tickets, and cherished memories of meeting the music legend. Many shared personal stories about how her music had influenced their lives, offering comfort in difficult times or serving as the soundtrack to their most treasured moments.

Prominent figures in the music industry expressed their sorrow and paid homage to Tina's contributions. Fellow artists lauded her groundbreaking influence, her ability to shatter glass ceilings and redefine the rules of the game, while maintaining her signature grace and humility.

News of Tina's passing flooded television screens and radio waves, with stations worldwide playing her most iconic hits, from 'What's Love Got to Do with It' to 'Proud Mary', turning the day into an impromptu global tribute to her illustrious career.

In the midst of this profound sadness, there was also a palpable undercurrent of admiration and celebration. The world did not just mourn Tina Turner; it celebrated her life, her resilience, and her indomitable spirit. It recognized the girl from Nutbush who had transformed into a global music sensation, acknowledging her challenges, her victories, and the lasting impact she made on countless lives.

Tina Turner's passing marked the end of a remarkable journey, one that began in a small town and ended in the hearts of millions. As we reflect on that day, we do not merely recall a moment of loss, but celebrate a life that was, in every sense, 'Simply the Best'. We remember a woman whose legacy will continue to inspire, whose music will continue to uplift, and whose spirit will forever echo in the annals of music history.

# PRT 12: Remembering Tina Turner

# Moment Nr. 51

## *Tributes to Tina: An Overview of Tributes from Fans and Fellow Musicians*

In the days following Tina Turner's passing, the world came together to honor a woman who had spent her lifetime inspiring, exciting, and revolutionizing the music industry. Her impact, reflected in tributes from fans and fellow musicians, served as a poignant testament to her enduring influence and her everlasting legacy.

Fans around the globe poured their hearts out on social media platforms, sharing personal anecdotes of how Tina's music had soundtracked their lives. From joyous celebrations to moments of solace, her voice had been a constant, reassuring presence. Homemade videos of fans singing along to 'Nutbush City Limits' in their living rooms or passionately reenacting the iconic dance routine from 'Proud Mary' were shared, bringing a sense of unity in the collective grief.

However, it wasn't just the fans that were mourning. The global music community stood together, paying homage to the woman who had redefined the boundaries of rock 'n' roll. Legendary musicians from different genres took to various platforms to express their admiration for Tina.

Mick Jagger, frontman of The Rolling Stones, called Tina "an electrifying performer and an incredible influence on music," recalling their memorable performance together in 1981. Beyoncé, who had often cited Tina as a major influence in her career, posted a heartfelt tribute, reflecting on Tina's inspiring journey and her groundbreaking achievements as a black woman in the music industry. Even younger artists, who had grown up listening to Tina's music, acknowledged the profound impact she had made on their musical journey.

Radio and television stations organized special tribute programs, dedicating entire days to playing Tina's discography and showing concert footage. Broadcasters interviewed her contemporaries, collaborators, and fans, weaving together a tapestry of stories that highlighted her radiant spirit and her immense talent.

Impromptu shrines appeared outside her former homes in the United States and Switzerland. Fans left flowers, letters, and mementos, turning these sites into vibrant memorials. Her star on the Hollywood Walk of Fame became a sea of roses and handwritten notes, a testament to the love and admiration of her fans.

Despite the undercurrent of sadness, the tributes were marked by a spirit of celebration, echoing Tina's own zest for life. They celebrated her strength, her resilience, and her remarkable journey from Anna Mae Bullock, a small-town girl, to Tina Turner, the undisputed queen of rock 'n' roll.

As we remember Tina, these tributes remind us of her enduring legacy. They paint a vivid portrait of a woman who was not just a music sensation but an icon of strength and resilience. The worldwide outpouring of love and admiration is a testament to the life and career of Tina Turner, a woman who was, and will always be, 'Simply the Best'.

# Moment Nr. 52

## Her Influence on Pop Culture: The Enduring Impact of Tina's Work on Music and Fashion

It is no small feat to be universally recognized as the "Queen of Rock 'n' Roll". Born Anna Mae Bullock, the girl who would become Tina Turner was destined to ignite a cultural phenomenon that would last long beyond her time. Tina Turner's unique blend of raw energy, soulful vocals, and empowering lyrics propelled her to global fame, indelibly imprinting her influence on the landscape of popular culture.

Her music, marked by a distinct fusion of rock and soul, redefined boundaries and inspired countless artists across multiple generations. From her early R&B hits with Ike Turner to her explosive solo career, Tina's work continually evolved, demonstrating her extraordinary musical versatility. Iconic tracks like "Proud Mary" and "What's Love Got to Do With It" became anthems of resilience and self-empowerment, striking a chord with audiences worldwide. Her innovative sounds and vibrant performances have left a lasting impact on the music industry, paving the way for artists like Beyoncé and Rihanna to break barriers in their own right.

Yet, Tina's influence extended well beyond the realms of music. With her unmistakable style, she revolutionized the fashion world. Her iconic look - the wild hair, the mini dresses, the high heels, and the sheer energy - sent shockwaves through the industry. She exuded confidence, strength, and undeniable allure, shattering conventional expectations of femininity and age. This was a woman who owned every inch of the stage, demonstrating a fierce independence that would inspire generations of women to embrace their own power.

Her indomitable spirit was mirrored in her off-stage persona, as she openly shared her life experiences. Tina's autobiography "I, Tina", which later became the basis for the film "What's Love Got to Do with It", showcased her courage in overcoming personal trauma, further solidifying her status as a role model. Her narrative of survival, resilience, and triumph resonated deeply with people around the world, transcending cultural, age, and gender divides.

As we reflect on her journey, it becomes abundantly clear that Tina Turner was much more than a music sensation - she was a cultural powerhouse. Her influence reverberates through the annals of pop culture, not just in the melodies that echo across radio waves or the striking images of her commanding the stage, but in the way she empowered others to embrace their individuality, their strength, and their spirit.

From a humble beginning in Nutbush, Tennessee, Tina Turner's influence has stretched across continents and decades. In her life and work, she encapsulated a celebration of resilience and power, leaving an indelible mark on the world that can still be felt today. Through her music, style, and sheer force of character, Tina Turner truly did become, 'Simply the Best'.

# Moment Nr. 53

## *Preserving Her Legacy: An Examination of Efforts to Remember and Honor Tina's Legacy*

As the curtains close on the remarkable life of Tina Turner, the reverberations of her powerful legacy continue to ring out. Born in the small town of Nutbush, Tennessee, Tina's journey took her to the pinnacle of international stardom, etching her name in the annals of music history. Yet her legacy extends far beyond her numerous chart-topping hits and her moniker as the "Queen of Rock 'n' Roll". It is etched in the hearts of millions who found solace, strength, and joy in her music and life story.

Tina's empowering narrative of survival and triumph over adversity is commemorated in various ways. Foremost among these is her 1986 autobiography, "I, Tina", co-written with Kurt Loder. The book serves as a testament to her resilience, offering a raw, unfiltered look at the hardships she endured and her ascent to fame. Later adapted into the Academy Award-nominated film "What's Love Got to Do with It", her story reached an even wider audience, continuing to inspire countless individuals across the globe.

In the music world, tributes abound. Posthumous covers of her songs are a testament to her enduring influence. Many of today's pop and rock icons cite her as a significant inspiration, underlining her lasting impact on the industry. Award shows and tribute concerts keep her music alive, allowing a new generation to experience the electrifying energy she brought to every performance.

Furthermore, institutions such as the Rock and Roll Hall of Fame, which inducted Tina both as a member of Ike & Tina Turner and as a solo artist, help preserve her musical legacy. The Tina Turner Museum at Flagg Grove School, her childhood schoolhouse, stands as a permanent reminder of her roots and the journey that transformed Anna Mae Bullock into the legendary Tina Turner.

Beyond the realm of music, her unique fashion style continues to influence designers, and her Buddhist practice underscores her philosophical legacy, with her spiritual journey captivating many who seek solace in her experiences.

But perhaps the most touching tributes come from the fans who adored her. Their stories about how Tina's music inspired them, provided comfort, or simply brought joy serve as the most poignant testament to her legacy. Murals, fan art, and personal stories shared on social media platforms are small but powerful reminders of the deep and personal connection her music fostered.

In every chord struck and every lyric sung, Tina Turner's legacy resonates. It is an enduring testament to her extraordinary talent, indomitable spirit, and her timeless message of resilience. As we continue to remember and honor Tina Turner, we are not only preserving the memory of an iconic music sensation but also celebrating a life that transcended adversity to inspire millions around the world. As such, her legacy will undoubtedly continue to flourish, touching the hearts of future generations just as profoundly as it has done ours.

# Moment Nr. 54

## *Tina Turner's Place in Music History: A Reflection on Tina's Significance in the Music Industry*

On November 26th, 1939, a star was born. This star was Anna Mae Bullock, known worldwide as Tina Turner, the Queen of Rock 'n' Roll. Her journey from the humble cotton fields of Nutbush, Tennessee, to global music sensation is not merely a biography; it is a testament to her enduring spirit, resilience, and boundless talent that continues to inspire and touch millions.

From the beginning, Tina's unique blend of soul, R&B, and rock music set her apart in the music industry. As the powerhouse voice of the Ike & Tina Turner Revue, she gained recognition for her raw, electrifying performances. Their rendition of "Proud Mary" remains a timeless classic, earning them a Grammy Award in 1972.

However, it was her resurgence in the 1980s as a solo artist that cemented Tina Turner's legendary status. Her album, "Private Dancer," brought her global acclaim, selling millions of copies worldwide. It spun out several hits, including the iconic "What's Love Got to Do with It," which topped the charts and won three Grammy Awards, including Record of the Year.

Tina's music career was extraordinary not just for the chart-topping hits but also for her ability to break barriers. As a Black woman in the music industry, she pushed boundaries, inspiring many other artists that followed. She was among the few women who thrived in the male-dominated genre of rock 'n' roll, and her success in her 40s defied the industry's ageism.

Moreover, Tina's high-energy performances and dynamic stage presence revolutionized the live music experience. Her concerts were more than mere performances; they were spectacular events that captivated audiences. As a consummate performer, her explosive energy, powerful vocals, and unrelenting passion encapsulated the essence of rock 'n' roll.

Tina's significance in the music industry is also marked by the awards and honors she received throughout her career. Her impressive tally of 12 Grammy Awards, including a Grammy Lifetime Achievement Award, is a testament to her talent and impact. Furthermore, her induction into the Rock and Roll Hall of Fame twice, both as a part of Ike & Tina Turner and as a solo artist, underscores her outstanding contribution to the genre.

But beyond the records, awards, and accolades, Tina Turner's lasting impact lies in her ability to connect with people through her music and her story. Her songs were not just melodic compositions but narratives of life, struggle, and triumph that resonated with listeners worldwide.

Tina Turner's place in music history is indisputable. As we reflect on her journey and contributions, we see a woman who transcended adversity to revolutionize the music industry, leaving an indelible mark. Her music and her story have inspired millions, and as we celebrate her life, we also honor the immense legacy that she leaves behind. To paraphrase one of her iconic songs, Tina Turner is, indeed, simply the best.

# Moment Nr. 55

## Her Influence on Future Generations: Discussion of Tina's Impact on Younger Artists and Her Enduring Legacy

Tina Turner's influence echoes through the corridors of time, bouncing off the walls of the past and the pillars of the present, before finding its home in the hearts of future generations. On the day of her birth, the world had yet to understand the magnitude of the gift it had been given. Born in Nutbush, Tennessee, Tina's humble beginnings would, against all odds, set her on a trajectory towards global stardom. A trajectory that would also chart the course for countless others who dared to dream and to defy.

Tina was a trailblazer. As the "Queen of Rock 'n' Roll," she broke barriers, defying societal norms and industry expectations. The music world was predominantly male, and rock 'n' roll was no exception. Yet, Tina emerged, her spirit unbowed, her presence undeniable, and her voice unmistakable. Her success was an inspiration, a beacon for younger artists – particularly women – demonstrating that there was space for them in this vibrant yet challenging world of rock music.

The likes of Beyoncé, Rihanna, and Adele have all publicly spoken about how Tina's electrifying stage performances, her unapologetic strength, and her raw, soulful voice have been a source of inspiration. These artists have echoed her sentiments, mirrored her powerful performances, and channeled her relentless resilience. Through them, and many others, Tina's influence endures, ensuring her spirit continues to pulsate through the veins of the music industry.

Her legacy also reaches beyond music. In the realm of fashion, Tina's bold and daring style has inspired generations. The iconic fringed dresses, high-heeled boots, and wild, tousled hair have found their place in the annals of fashion history, and have been echoed on stages and red carpets worldwide. Her fashion statements were as powerful as her music, underlining her unique brand of fearlessness and individuality.

Moreover, Tina Turner's life story, a testament to resilience in the face of adversity, continues to inspire millions. Her autobiography, "I, Tina," and the subsequent biopic, "What's Love Got to Do with It," have left an indelible mark, documenting her journey from an abusive relationship to reclaiming her life and career. Through her candid narration of her experiences, Tina gave a voice to many who felt unheard and offered hope to those in despair.

In Tina Turner, the world found more than a musician. They found a fighter, a survivor, an icon. Her voice gave sound to their emotions, her life gave a mirror to their struggles, and her success offered a vision of their hopes. As we remember her on this significant day, we celebrate not only the birth of a musical legend but also the dawn of a legacy that continues to empower, inspire, and endure in the hearts of countless fans and artists alike. Tina Turner was not just a star; she was a galaxy of hope and inspiration, her light reaching far into the future, touching lives yet to be born.

# Moment Nr. 56

## *Her Relationship with Her Children: Exploring her bond with her sons, Craig and Ronnie*

In the symphony of Tina Turner's life, amidst the crescendo of her music and the pulsating rhythm of her career, there was a soft, steady harmony that played in the background. This was the melody of motherhood, the tender bond she shared with her sons, Craig and Ronnie.

Born in the small town of Nutbush, Tennessee, Tina was no stranger to hardship and struggle. Yet, despite the storms that would batter her life, she remained a steadfast beacon for her sons. Her unwavering love for them was as clear and radiant as her voice, as strong and sturdy as the chords of her songs.

Her first son, Craig, was the product of a relationship with Raymond Hill, a saxophonist for the Kings of Rhythm band. Though their relationship was brief, it resulted in the birth of a son, a joy Tina would carry with her throughout her tumultuous years with Ike Turner.

Ronnie Turner, her second son, was born of her union with Ike Turner. Despite their troubled marriage, the birth of Ronnie brought a semblance of peace and happiness to Tina's life. Her sons became her anchor, her safe harbor amid life's turbulent waves.

Tina Turner, the 'Queen of Rock and Roll', was an extraordinary talent. But she was also an extraordinary mother. Her strength, resilience, and dedication were not just manifest on the stage, but also in her role as a mother. Even as her career demanded much of her time and energy, she ensured that her sons felt loved and valued.

The press rarely glimpsed this side of Tina, the private, family-focused woman behind the dazzling public persona. But it was this aspect of her life, this unshakable commitment to her children, that revealed the true depth of her character. Tina was not just an incredible artist and performer; she was a compassionate and caring mother.

Her sons were central to her life, her heartbeats made tangible. Even in her last moments, the love for her sons shone through, a testament to the strength of her maternal bond. She left behind a legacy of music, yes, but also a legacy of love, of a mother's fierce and unwavering affection for her children.

In remembering Tina Turner, we remember her music, her electrifying performances, her profound impact on the world of music. But let us also remember the woman who held her sons close, who sang lullabies before singing anthems, who was, at her core, a loving mother. This, too, is the legacy of Tina Turner, a testament to her strength, her courage, and her boundless love.

# Moment Nr. 57

## The Mystery of Her Middle Name: The Story Behind 'Mae'

Amidst the monumental feats and significant moments of Tina Turner's life, there lies a quiet yet compelling tale – the story of her middle name 'Mae'.

Born Anna Mae Bullock on November 26, 1939, in Nutbush, Tennessee, 'Mae' was not just a name; it was a symbol of her roots, a gentle nod to her humble beginnings before she took the world by storm. Tina Turner, the indomitable icon of music, began her journey as Anna Mae Bullock, the small-town girl with a voice that held the promise of stardom.

The name 'Mae' came from her mother, Zelma Priscilla Currie, who named her after a beloved relative. In the rural simplicity of Nutbush, amidst the cotton fields and country roads, 'Mae' was a name that held a charm and character reflective of the landscape and people.

While the name 'Tina' was a brand, a dynamic and electrifying persona that shone under the spotlight, 'Mae' was her anchor, her connection to her roots. It served as a poignant reminder of her initial years, marked by a blend of dreams, struggles, and familial ties.

Yet, the name 'Mae' was more than just a link to her past. It also served as a vital part of her transformation – a transformation that led to the creation of a legendary figure, Tina Turner. When she stepped onto the stage as Tina, she brought with her the strength, resilience, and humility that 'Mae' signified. Her middle name, though not often in the limelight, played a crucial role in shaping the artist and woman she became.

'Mae' eventually faded into the background as Tina's stardom rose, but it remained an integral part of her identity, hidden but not forgotten. Even as she charmed audiences worldwide with her powerful performances and striking personality, the echoes of 'Mae' were always there, subtly woven into her music, her life, and her journey.

As we celebrate the life of Tina Turner, the vibrant force of nature who transformed the music industry, let us also remember Anna Mae Bullock, the spirited young girl from Nutbush who dared to dream. She held onto her dreams and, with courage in her heart and song on her lips, she ventured into the world, ready to leave her mark. And she did, not just as Tina Turner, but also as Anna Mae Bullock, a name that signifies her remarkable journey from a small-town girl to a global superstar.

So, in the name 'Mae' lies the essence of Tina Turner. It is a testament to her journey, her transformation, and her ties to her past. It reminds us that behind the legendary Tina Turner, there was, and always will be, a touch of Anna Mae – the girl from Nutbush, Tennessee.

# Moment Nr. 58

## *Reinvention in the '80s: How She Staged One of the Most Remarkable Comebacks in Music History*

In the panorama of music history, certain events forever shift the terrain. In the 1980s, such a seismic event took place - the astounding resurgence of Tina Turner. This wasn't just a comeback; it was a renaissance that highlighted her resilience, talent, and indomitable spirit.

By the late 1970s, Tina Turner, already a household name due to her successful partnership with Ike Turner, was embarking on a challenging solo career. Battling personal turmoil and professional setbacks, she was considered a star whose light had started to dim. But those who knew Tina understood one thing - never underestimate her.

The dawn of the 1980s marked a new era, not just in music but also in Tina's life and career. The small-town girl, now a seasoned performer, wasn't done yet. She had more to give, more to show, and she did that in spectacular fashion.

Her reinvention began with a renewed focus on her music. Working with different producers, Tina started exploring a fusion of rock, pop, and soul. This new direction led to the creation of "Private Dancer", her fifth solo album. The record's reception was nothing short of a phenomenon, selling millions of copies and solidifying Tina's place as a leading figure in the music industry.

Tina Turner, the woman who once sang at small gigs in St. Louis, was now captivating audiences at packed arenas around the world. Her vibrant performances and unique voice enthralled a new generation of fans. Yet, she remained quintessentially Tina - a powerhouse performer radiating strength, passion, and authenticity.

The '80s was also a decade of recognition for Tina. Awards and accolades started pouring in, acknowledging not just her music but her extraordinary comeback. She won multiple Grammys, including Record of the Year for "What's Love Got to Do with It" - a song that became an anthem for her resurgence.

Tina's reinvention was more than just a professional accomplishment; it was a personal triumph. Despite the odds, she rose from the ashes of her past, not only reclaiming her place in the music industry but also shaping it in her image. Her resilience inspired countless others, particularly women, proving that it's never too late to reinvent oneself, to reach for success, and to turn life's lows into powerful comeback stories.

As we remember Tina Turner, let us not forget the '80s - a decade that witnessed one of the most remarkable comebacks in music history. It is a testament to her character, to her unyielding spirit, and to her undeniable talent. This era in her life and career showcases her determination to remain "Simply the Best", embodying the tenacity of a woman who refused to fade into obscurity. Her legacy continues to inspire, reminding us that every setback can be a setup for a comeback, a lesson that Tina Turner embodied in her spectacular resurgence.

# Moment Nr. 59

## *Touring the World: The Significance of Her Global Tours and Their Impact on Her Career*

Tina Turner was a force of nature, and nowhere was her uncontainable spirit more apparent than on the global stage. With an electrifying blend of powerful vocals, unyielding energy, and intense charisma, Tina left a lasting impact on countless fans across continents. The significance of her worldwide tours transcends mere performance - they marked the global embrace of a unique talent, the universal resonance of her music, and a pivotal elevation in her extraordinary career.

Born on November 26, 1939, in the small town of Nutbush, Tennessee, Anna Mae Bullock – the world would later come to know her as Tina Turner – possessed a voice that was destined to reach beyond the confines of her humble beginnings. The world tours served as a testament to the profound reach of this remarkable woman's talent.

Tina's global tours started gaining momentum in the 1980s, a decade which marked a magnificent revival of her career. She was no longer a regional sensation; Tina Turner became a worldwide phenomenon. From Europe to Asia, North America to Australia, Tina's music reverberated in every corner of the globe, transcending borders and cultural differences. She was the girl from Nutbush who grew up to serenade the world.

Perhaps the most legendary of these tours was the "Break Every Rule World Tour" (1987–1988), which broke attendance records and remains one of the most significant concert tours in music history. The tour witnessed Tina performing to packed stadiums, often with capacity exceeding 100,000. Each show was a celebration, not just of her music, but also of her triumphant resurgence against all odds.

Through these global tours, Tina established herself as a live music icon. Her concerts were not just about singing; they were about performing, about connecting, about sharing her music and her journey with millions of fans. She stood on stage, often for hours, pouring every ounce of her energy into her performances. It was her way of giving back the love she received from fans worldwide.

The importance of her global tours was not limited to her career's ascendance. They were instrumental in shaping her legacy. The world got to witness firsthand the resilience, the talent, and the sheer force of will that defined Tina Turner. Each concert was a testament to her strength, her resolve, and her passion for music.

As we remember Tina Turner, it is vital to acknowledge the extraordinary impact of her global tours. They encapsulated the essence of her journey - from Nutbush to the world, from adversity to triumph, from Anna Mae Bullock to Tina Turner. In touring the world, she brought the world closer, leaving a trail of musical brilliance and inspiring stories of strength and perseverance. The echoes of her voice in stadiums worldwide remind us of a legend who was born to perform and born to inspire - a legend who was, and always will be, "Simply the Best".

# Moment Nr. 60

## Tina's Fashion Impact: An Exploration of Tina's Iconic Style and its Influence on the Fashion World

November 26, 1939, marked the dawn of a life that would echo through the annals of music and fashion history, igniting a flame that would illuminate the world. Anna Mae Bullock, known to the world as Tina Turner, entered the world in Nutbush, Tennessee, not yet aware of the magnitude of her destined impact.

From a young age, Tina exuded a vibrant energy that couldn't be confined to the small town she called home. A vivid beacon of fiery spirit, her personality echoed the strength and resilience that would come to define her life and career.

As her musical journey began in earnest, Tina's style was as influential as her voice. Her signature style—wild hair, short skirts, high heels—paved the way for women in the music industry and made her a fashion icon. Her presence on stage was as electrifying as her performances; her style a rebellious, unapologetic celebration of femininity, empowerment, and freedom.

Tina's influence in the fashion world was monumental, prompting a seismic shift in norms. Her distinctive look became a symbol of audacious femininity and strength, pushing boundaries and setting a precedent for future generations. It was this brazen confidence and unique flair that not only etched Tina's name in the annals of fashion but also helped shape the visual vocabulary of rock 'n' roll itself.

Her audacious mini dresses, paired with fringed leather jackets, defied the conventions of modesty and respectability. She was the picture of daring and defiance, her garments reflective of her grit and resilience. No doubt, Tina was instrumental in transforming the rock 'n' roll aesthetic, shifting it from a male-dominated sphere to a realm where women could be fierce, strong, and unequivocally themselves.

Yet, despite the glitz and the glamour, Tina remained true to her roots. She never lost the spark of the Nutbush girl who dared to dream. This was evident in the way she gracefully carried her personal and stage persona, unifying her heritage and the unshake-able spirit of her home town with her international fame.

A study of Tina Turner's fashion impact transcends mere aesthetics. It unveils the narrative of a woman who used fashion as a form of self-expression, rebellion, and empowerment, challenging societal norms and encouraging others to do the same. To witness Tina in her prime was to watch a woman claiming her space, not just in the music world, but in society at large. Her legacy, thus, is one that continues to inspire, and resonate with individuals across the globe.

In a career spanning more than half a century, Tina Turner moved from humble beginnings to the pinnacle of global stardom, forever leaving her mark on the world. Her life was a testament to the enduring power of resilience and determination. Today, as we remember the unforgettable Tina Turner, we celebrate not only the iconic artist, but the fashion trendsetter, the trailblazer, and the woman whose spirit never waned, reflecting the truth of her hit song, she was indeed "Simply the Best".

# Moment Nr. 61

## *The Philanthropic Side of Tina: An Examination of Tina's charitable acts and causes she supported*

The birth of Anna Mae Bullock on November 26, 1939, in Nutbush, Tennessee, heralded the arrival of a resilient spirit destined to become Tina Turner, the Queen of Rock 'n' Roll. Beyond her awe-inspiring career as a music icon, Tina had a profound influence off-stage, too. She exemplified grace, resilience, and most significantly, her relentless philanthropic spirit marked an enduring legacy.

Tina was not only a superstar on stage but also in the arena of charity and philanthropy. Over the years, she supported a myriad of causes, leveraging her fame to bring about change. Her philanthropic endeavors reflected her compassionate heart, just as her soulful music mirrored her indomitable spirit.

One cause particularly close to Tina's heart was Children Beyond, a music project she collaborated on with Regula Curti and Dechen Shak-Dagsay. Aiming to unite cultures and promote peace, they released an album whose proceeds went to support children affected by war, helping them attain education and stability. This charitable act highlighted Tina's deep-rooted belief in the transformative power of education and her dedication to creating a better world for the next generation.

As an avid follower of Buddhism, Tina was also known for her spiritual philanthropy. She shared her journey through her faith with the world, inspiring many with her strength and resilience, most notably seen in her autobiographical book, "Happiness Becomes You: A Guide to Changing Your Life for Good". The book was a testament to her faith's empowering impact on her life and served as a beacon of hope for those navigating their own adversities.

Tina also fervently supported the fight against tuberculosis, lending her voice to the Stop TB Partnership. Her contribution to this cause was vital in spreading awareness and garnering necessary funding to combat this deadly disease. It was a reflection of her belief in the power of health as a fundamental right for all.

Moreover, Tina never forgot her roots. She showed her love for Nutbush by investing in her hometown, promoting various projects aimed at revitalizing the local community and preserving its cultural heritage. She ensured that Nutbush continued to be a source of inspiration and development for its residents and visitors alike.

Tina Turner was not only a globally recognized artist but also a woman with a heart as golden as her voice. Her philanthropic journey was as extraordinary as her music career, a testament to her immense capacity for empathy, kindness, and love. She used her platform to shine a light on issues close to her heart, never hesitating to lend her voice and resources to effect change.

As we remember Tina Turner, the beloved music icon, let us also honor her legacy of giving, her humanitarian spirit that continues to reverberate. She was a beacon of strength, resilience, and benevolence, embodying the adage that we rise by lifting others. As the title of our tribute suggests, in every sense of the term, Tina Turner was, and will always be, "Simply the Best".

# Moment Nr. 62

## *Her Unshakeable Spirit: Understanding Tina's Resilience and the Source of her Strength*

On November 26, 1939, a remarkable journey began in the small town of Nutbush, Tennessee. The birth of Anna Mae Bullock, later known worldwide as Tina Turner, marked the inception of a life that would inspire millions through not only her music but also her unyielding spirit.

Growing up in Nutbush, Tina endured hardships that shaped her resilience. Her parents' early departure from her life and the trials she encountered instilled in her a robust determination that would become the bedrock of her unshakeable spirit.

In her early career, Tina confronted adversity head-on, persevering despite challenging circumstances. As a Black woman in the music industry in the 1960s, she navigated a landscape fraught with racial tension and inequality. Nevertheless, she rose above these societal barriers, her powerful voice shattering glass ceilings, demonstrating that talent and determination could overcome even the harshest of obstacles.

The source of Tina's strength was multi-faceted. Notably, her spirituality played a significant role. Tina became a devout follower of Buddhism in the mid-1970s, finding solace and resilience in its teachings. Her Buddhist practice, particularly chanting Nam Myoho Renge Kyo, became a wellspring of strength that helped her weather the tumultuous storms of her life. She often credited her faith for providing her the courage and tenacity to leave her abusive marriage and rebuild her career.

Tina's unwavering dedication to her art was another testament to her unshakeable spirit. Even in the face of personal difficulties, she remained relentless in her pursuit of her musical career. Her second act in the 1980s, leading to her triumphant solo career, marked an incredible comeback, reinforcing her status as a symbol of tenacity and resilience.

Above all, Tina's strength came from a profound place of self-love and self-belief. Despite the hardships she encountered, she never allowed her past to define her. Instead, she channeled her experiences into an unyielding resolve to forge a better path for herself, becoming an inspirational figure for millions worldwide.

Even after her retirement, Tina's spirit remained strong. Her story continued to inspire through her musical "Tina: The Tina Turner Musical" and her documentary "Tina," bringing her journey of resilience to a new generation. Her enduring strength, seen in her public battle with health issues, underscored her mantra of resilience that defined her life: "I don't regret anything. Life is a journey."

As we remember Tina Turner, we celebrate not just an extraordinary artist, but an extraordinarily resilient woman. Her legacy is her unshakeable spirit, her unbowed resolve that reverberates through her music and life. From Nutbush to global stardom, Tina Turner was not just "Simply the Best"; she was simply unstoppable.

# Moment Nr. 63

## *The Distinctive Turner Voice: Analyzing the Uniqueness and Power of Her Vocal Prowess*

In the humble town of Nutbush, Tennessee, on November 26, 1939, a voice was born that would reverberate through the hearts and souls of millions. That voice, a delicate yet potent blend of power and warmth, belonged to the girl who would become the legendary Tina Turner. The birth of Anna Mae Bullock heralded the dawn of a life destined to shift the tectonic plates of the global music scene.

Tina's voice was a distinctive marvel, an embodiment of her resilient spirit. It was like a symphony played on the strings of a finely-tuned instrument, resounding with notes of trials and triumphs, echoing the blues and soul, with an undercurrent of gospel, a nod to her early years singing in the church choir.

Tina's voice was characterized by her unique ability to balance power with sensitivity. She could belt out high-energy rock anthems like "Proud Mary" and "Simply the Best," setting stadiums alight with her radiant, raw energy. Yet, she could also infuse her vocals with poignant vulnerability on heart-wrenching ballads like "Private Dancer," touching listeners to their core.

The soul of Tina's vocal prowess lay in her unabashed emotion. It was as though each word she sang was soaked in the richness of her life experiences. From her tumultuous early life, marked by family abandonment and hardship, to her explosive rise to global stardom, Tina's vocal depth was the canvas on which her life's story was painted.

Her voice wasn't just heard, it was felt. It resonated with audiences because it was honest and real. It became the emblem of her transformation from a Southern girl with dreams to an international music icon, leaving an indelible mark on the annals of pop culture.

What set Tina apart wasn't just the power of her voice, but the way she used it. She pushed the limits of her vocal range, experimented with different genres, and never shied away from pushing her own boundaries. She adapted her vocal style from soul and R&B to rock and pop, proving her versatility and cementing her status as a musical chameleon.

Her tenacity and resilience shone through her performances, revealing a woman who, despite the adversities she faced, never let them define her. Instead, she used her trials as fuel to drive her forward, to imbue her performances with a passion and fervor that few could match.

When we celebrate Tina Turner, we pay homage to more than just her unmatched career or her countless hits. We honor a voice that defined an era, a voice that dared to be distinctive, powerful, and genuine. We remember a voice that conveyed strength and vulnerability, hardship and triumph, all woven into the same melody.

Tina Turner, born Anna Mae Bullock, arrived into this world in the small, close-knit town of Nutbush, a girl destined to become an international sensation. Yet, through all her success, she remained grounded, with a voice that was as authentic as the soil of the Tennessee town where her journey began.

In the end, we celebrate not just the voice of Tina Turner, but the woman behind it – a woman whose life and voice inspired millions, a woman who was, in every sense, Simply the Best.

# Moment Nr. 64

## *Staying Private in Public Life: How Tina Balanced Her Private and Public Lives*

When a tiny spark of life ignited in Nutbush, Tennessee, on November 26, 1939, no one could predict the luminous star it would become. That spark was Anna Mae Bullock, who we came to adore as Tina Turner, a woman whose resilience and talent would influence generations. Born into a humble, challenging life, Tina rose to become a global music phenomenon, her compelling voice touching millions.

Being in the public eye can be a double-edged sword, and few knew this better than Tina Turner. As her star rose and her life became fodder for public consumption, Tina displayed remarkable grace and wisdom in maintaining a careful balance between her public persona and private life.

Tina's public life was a whirlwind of studio sessions, electrifying performances, and world tours. The energy and vitality she brought to her performances enchanted audiences, earning her the moniker, "The Queen of Rock 'n' Roll." She engaged with her fans with the openness and warmth that were the hallmarks of her onstage persona.

Yet, beneath the dazzling spotlight, Tina managed to carve out a private life that was remarkably ordinary and grounded. She maintained an air of mystery around her personal life, revealing just enough to satisfy public curiosity while keeping the intimate details shielded from prying eyes. This fine balancing act was no small feat, and it demonstrated Tina's respect for her own privacy, an attribute often rare in celebrities of her stature.

Away from the bright lights and the loud applause, Tina found her solace in everyday life. She developed a profound love for gardening, spending hours tending to her home's lush greenery. She also had a deep interest in spirituality, notably Buddhism, which played an instrumental role in guiding her through the tumultuous moments in her life.

Even in the face of personal turmoil, Tina managed to keep her private struggles separate from her public persona. She was a master at compartmentalizing, allowing her to work through her issues privately while continuing to captivate audiences with her unwavering energy and talent.

Tina Turner was a testament to the fact that one can have a high-profile life yet maintain a private persona. It was her innate understanding of the need for personal space and her boundary-setting skills that enabled her to achieve this balance.

Her ability to maintain this dichotomy between her private and public lives further amplified the respect and admiration she received from her fans. Her story has become a beacon for artists who grapple with maintaining their own personal space amidst the demands of fame. It serves as a reminder that, even in the public eye, one's private life should be respected and cherished.

In celebrating the remarkable life of Tina Turner, we acknowledge her incredible journey from a small-town girl to an international icon. Yet, we must also commend her for the often overlooked but equally critical accomplishment - maintaining her privacy amidst the chaos of a public life.

As we remember Tina today, we honor not only her exceptional talent and resilience but also her wisdom and grace in balancing her private and public lives. Her life stands as a testament to the fact that, no matter how high one soars, staying grounded is crucial. In every sense, Tina Turner truly was, and will always remain, "Simply the Best".

# Moment Nr. 65

## The Art of Performance - An analysis of Tina's electrifying stage presence and performances

Tina Turner, born Anna Mae Bullock on November 26, 1939, sprouted from the fertile soils of Nutbush, Tennessee. The small town, cradled in the cotton fields of the American South, would be the first witness to a star in the making, a force of nature named Tina Turner.

Little did Nutbush know that the wide-eyed girl singing in the choir at Spring Hill Baptist Church would transform into a dazzling diamond that shone brighter than the Sun. Tina Turner, with her iconic voice and powerful stage presence, would one day redefine the very essence of performance.

It was in this humble town that Tina Turner's enchanting journey began. Her birth marked the beginning of a journey filled with power, passion, and undeniable perseverance that led her to become a global music sensation.

As a child, Tina found solace and liberation in music. The rhythm and soul of gospel tunes at her local church awakened her inherent musical prowess. Yet, the church choir was just the prelude to the symphony her life would become. Even then, little Anna Mae exuded an energy and a vibrancy that were simply infectious, compelling the congregation to sway along with her heartfelt hymns.

Tina Turner's stage performances were a testament to her extraordinary spirit. They were a spectacle of raw emotion and exceptional talent that left audiences captivated and yearning for more. Every twist of her hips, every flip of her wild mane, and each belted note was a testament to her indomitable will. Tina didn't just perform; she poured her heart and soul into every note, every dance move, taking audiences on a soul-stirring journey that transcended the realm of music into an experience of raw, untamed emotion.

When Tina Turner took the stage, the world watched in awe. Her fierce spirit was as captivating as her voice, radiating an intensity that was electric, raw, and thoroughly hypnotic. Her performances became a beacon of resilience and empowerment, inspiring millions around the globe. In her presence, music was more than melody and rhythm; it was a language of liberation, a testament to the human spirit's resilience.

Beyond her captivating voice and thrilling stage presence, Tina Turner embodied strength and resilience. The trials she faced, both personally and professionally, would have toppled many, but not Tina. She transformed each challenge into a stepping stone, rising ever higher, ever stronger. It was this unyielding spirit, reflected in her powerful performances, that made Tina a symbol of empowerment and endurance.

Tina Turner's birth marked the dawn of an era—an era of relentless resilience, timeless music, and riveting performances. From the quaint town of Nutbush to stages around the world, Tina Turner created a legacy that will echo in the halls of music history forever. Her life and career were not merely a collection of noteworthy moments; they were a symphony of resilience, talent, and unyielding determination. It's this symphony we celebrate today, remembering Tina Turner, a woman who was, and forever will be, simply the best.

# Moment Nr. 66

## *Her Affinity for Switzerland - A look into why Tina chose to make Switzerland her home*

Tina Turner, born Anna Mae Bullock on November 26, 1939, in the small town of Nutbush, Tennessee, was destined to become a global sensation. Tina's story, though marked by triumphant success on international stages, always looped back to her simple beginnings and the charm of a close-knit community.

However, there was another place, far removed from Nutbush's cotton fields and the hustle and bustle of American music cities, that captured Tina's heart. Nestled in the heart of Europe, with the Alps as its crown and Lake Zurich its jewel, Switzerland became the place Tina Turner would call home.

In 1994, Tina moved into a stunning chateau, fondly named the "Chateau Algonquin", in Küsnacht, a municipality on Lake Zurich. With its serene landscapes, captivating sceneries, and tranquil life-style, Switzerland seemed to reflect a quiet strength and peaceful resilience much like Tina herself.

In interviews, Tina often expressed her profound love for Switzerland, describing it as a haven where she could find solitude, tranquility, and genuine happiness. In contrast to her electrifying performances, her life in Switzerland was a symphony of quiet moments and serene landscapes, a place where she could recharge and reflect.

Tina Turner, the queen of rock 'n roll, traded in her high heels for hiking boots, exploring the captivating Swiss landscapes, inhaling the fresh Alpine air, and immersing herself in the peaceful rhythm of Swiss life. It was a choice that spoke volumes about her affinity for balance and her appreciation for the quiet strength and resilience that life away from the spotlight offered.

The serene ambiance of Switzerland allowed Tina to engage with her surroundings, her thoughts, and her music in a way that was deeply personal and fulfilling. Her chateau, overlooking Lake Zurich, became a sanctuary where she could revel in her successes, heal from her struggles, and rejoice in the extraordinary journey she had embarked upon.

In Switzerland, Tina found more than just a home; she found a community that embraced her, a landscape that enchanted her, and a tranquility that mirrored her own inner peace. Even after becoming a Swiss citizen in 2013, Tina never forgot her Nutbush roots; rather, she bridged her humble beginnings with her global stardom, linking the cotton fields of Tennessee with the Alpine meadows of Switzerland.

Tina's story is not only a chronicle of a music sensation but also a narrative about finding home - a place where one's heart is at peace. The story of Tina Turner and her affinity for Switzerland is a testa- ment to her ability to seek balance, tranquility, and peace amidst a life that was often lived in the fast lane.

On her 83rd birthday, we celebrate not just Tina Turner, the global superstar, but also Tina, the woman who found her sanctuary in the heart of Switzerland. Her journey from Nutbush to Küsnacht is a beautiful symphony of her life, echoing resilience, strength, and an unending quest for inner peace.

# Moment Nr. 67

## Her Affinity for Switzerland - A look into why Tina chose to make Switzerland her home

Tina Turner, born Anna Mae Bullock on November 26, 1939, in the small town of Nutbush, Tennessee, was destined to become a global sensation. Tina's story, though marked by triumphant success on international stages, always looped back to her simple beginnings and the charm of a close-knit community.

However, there was another place, far removed from Nutbush's cotton fields and the hustle and bustle of American music cities, that captured Tina's heart. Nestled in the heart of Europe, with the Alps as its crown and Lake Zurich its jewel, Switzerland became the place Tina Turner would call home.

In 1994, Tina moved into a stunning chateau, fondly named the "Chateau Algonquin", in Küsnacht, a municipality on Lake Zurich. With its serene landscapes, captivating sceneries, and tranquil life-style, Switzerland seemed to reflect a quiet strength and peaceful resilience much like Tina herself.

In interviews, Tina often expressed her profound love for Switzerland, describing it as a haven where she could find solitude, tranquility, and genuine happiness. In contrast to her electrifying performances, her life in Switzerland was a symphony of quiet moments and serene landscapes, a place where she could recharge and reflect.

Tina Turner, the queen of rock 'n roll, traded in her high heels for hiking boots, exploring the captivating Swiss landscapes, inhaling the fresh Alpine air, and immersing herself in the peaceful rhythm of Swiss life. It was a choice that spoke volumes about her affinity for balance and her appreciation for the quiet strength and resilience that life away from the spotlight offered.

The serene ambiance of Switzerland allowed Tina to engage with her surroundings, her thoughts, and her music in a way that was deeply personal and fulfilling. Her chateau, overlooking Lake Zurich, became a sanctuary where she could revel in her successes, heal from her struggles, and rejoice in the extraordinary journey she had embarked upon.

In Switzerland, Tina found more than just a home; she found a community that embraced her, a landscape that enchanted her, and a tranquility that mirrored her own inner peace. Even after becoming a Swiss citizen in 2013, Tina never forgot her Nutbush roots; rather, she bridged her humble beginnings with her global stardom, linking the cotton fields of Tennessee with the Alpine meadows of Switzerland.

Tina's story is not only a chronicle of a music sensation but also a narrative about finding home - a place where one's heart is at peace. The story of Tina Turner and her affinity for Switzerland is a testament to her ability to seek balance, tranquility, and peace amidst a life that was often lived in the fast lane.

On her 83rd birthday, we celebrate not just Tina Turner, the global superstar, but also Tina, the woman who found her sanctuary in the heart of Switzerland. Her journey from Nutbush to Küsnacht is a beautiful symphony of her life, echoing resilience, strength, and an unending quest for inner peace.

# Moment Nr. 68

## *Influence on Music Videos - Understanding the impact Tina had on the evolution of music videos*

On November 26, 1939, the world witnessed the birth of a woman who would redefine the music industry in ways more than one. Tina Turner, a small-town girl from Nutbush, Tennessee, was not just a phenomenal singer; she was a trailblazer, a visionary, and a woman whose influence spanned beyond music and impacted its visual counterpart - the music video.

The advent of the music video in the early 1980s provided artists a new medium to engage with their audience. At the forefront of this transformative wave was Tina Turner, whose dynamic presence and indomitable spirit found an innovative platform in music videos. Through this new medium, she combined her powerful vocals, electrifying stage presence, and compelling storytelling, providing audiences a visual experience that perfectly complemented her music.

Take for example her iconic video for "What's Love Got to Do With It". It was in this visually stimulating story that Tina Turner crafted an image of strength and resilience. Her character, a woman discovering her independence and personal power, resonated with millions worldwide, creating a narrative that stretched beyond the boundaries of the song.

As her career progressed, Tina's influence on music videos became more apparent. With videos like "Private Dancer" and "We Don't Need Another Hero", Tina Turner pushed the envelope, evolving from a singer performing on stage to a captivating storyteller. Each video was a mini-movie, showcasing her acting abilities, creative ideas, and of course, her unparalleled musical talent.

Moreover, it was through these music videos that Tina Turner challenged societal norms. She was unafraid to present herself as a strong, confident woman, often cast in empowering roles. Whether it was her role as a dystopian queen in "Mad Max: Beyond Thunderdome" or a passionate performer in "Private Dancer", Tina challenged stereotypes, redefining what it meant to be a female artist in the music industry.

The impact of Tina Turner's contribution to the music video medium is immeasurable. Her work inspired and paved the way for countless artists who followed, fostering creativity and promoting diversity in a medium that was still finding its footing.

On this day, as we remember Tina Turner, we don't just celebrate a legendary singer; we honor a pioneer. We honor a woman who used her talent and her vision to change the way we perceive and experience music. From her humble beginnings in Nutbush to her global influence on music and its visual counterpart, Tina Turner's life and career are a testament to the power of innovation, resilience, and creativity.

As we commemorate the 83 pivotal moments of her life and career, we recognize the undeniable influence she had on the evolution of music videos, a legacy that will continue to inspire future generations. Today, we salute Tina Turner, a woman who was truly, undeniably, 'simply the best'.

# Moment Nr. 69

## *Living Buddhism - The role of Buddhism in shaping Tina's life Philosophy and Outlook.*

On November 26, 1939, a star was born, a beacon of hope and resilience who would go on to inspire millions across the globe - Tina Turner. The girl from Nutbush, Tennessee, would not only revolutionize the music industry but would also shape a philosophical outlook that resonated with her legion of fans. An integral part of this philosophy was her adherence to Buddhism, a faith that played a crucial role in shaping her life.

Tina Turner's association with Buddhism began during one of the most tumultuous periods in her life. Facing personal and professional hardships, she found solace in the teachings of the Nichiren School of Buddhism. The religion's emphasis on overcoming challenges, creating value in any situation, and the power of inner transformation deeply resonated with Tina.

The practice of chanting 'Nam-myoho-renge-kyo' became a cornerstone of Tina's life. This mantra, central to Nichiren Buddhism, underscores the belief in the inherent dignity and potential of all life. Tina embraced this philosophy, using it as a source of strength and a vehicle for change. She often attributed her comeback in the '80s to the fortitude she derived from her Buddhist practice.

Buddhism also shaped Tina's worldview, teaching her the principles of compassion, gratitude, and interconnectedness. These principles were reflected not just in her personal life but in her music as well. Songs like "We Don't Need Another Hero" and "What's Love Got to Do With It" exuded a sense of empathy and resilience that was testament to her Buddhist beliefs.

Tina's faith in Buddhism wasn't a matter of ritualistic practices; it was a way of life. It was about harnessing the power within to effect positive change in her life and in the world around her. This perspective was beautifully encapsulated in her statement, "I'm a Buddhist-Baptist. My training will always be Baptist, but my philosophy will always be Buddhism."

As we commemorate Tina Turner's birth, we do not just celebrate an iconic musician but a resilient woman whose spiritual journey has been as inspiring as her musical journey. Her commitment to Buddhism and its principles of compassion, resilience, and self-empowerment was as much a part of her persona as her electrifying performances and soulful music.

Today, as we reflect on the 83 pivotal moments in Tina Turner's life and career, we acknowledge the profound influence Buddhism had on this remarkable woman. It was her guiding light in times of darkness, her source of strength in the face of adversity, and her path to inner peace and happiness. The Tina Turner we remember today was not just the Queen of Rock 'n' Roll; she was a woman who lived her truth, undeterred by challenges, ever resilient, and always inspiring. She was, and will always be, 'simply the best.'

# Moment Nr. 70

## *Dealing with Loss - Insights into how Tina dealt with the loss of her son Craig*

Tina Turner, born Anna Mae Bullock on November 26, 1939, went from humble beginnings to superstardom, overcoming numerous adversities and challenges on her journey. One of these trials was the devastating loss of her son, Craig Raymond Turner, in 2018. Craig was Tina's first child, a beacon of light in her life, and his loss left an indelible mark on her.

Tina's strength was always her defining trait, both on stage and off. But it was her private handling of Craig's loss that showed us another facet of her courage, a raw, internal fortitude that was as powerful as her most passionate performances.

When speaking about her son's passing, Tina displayed an unshakeable bravery, an example of hcr innate resilience and inner strength. Instead of succumbing to despair, she chose to focus on her son's life, cherishing the moments of joy they shared. This ability to celebrate life in the face of heartbreaking loss is a testament to Tina's indomitable spirit.

Tina openly attributed her strength in dealing with such a profound personal tragedy to her Buddhist beliefs. She leaned into her faith during this period of pain and loss, using the principles of

Buddhism to navigate her grief. The practice of chanting, a central tenet of her Buddhist faith, provided her with a source of solace and comfort.

While the pain of losing a child is immeasurable, Tina was determined to turn her personal grief into a broader message of hope. In interviews following Craig's death, she encouraged those dealing with similar experiences to seek help, expressing the importance of addressing mental health concerns.

The loss of her son Craig was undoubtedly one of the most difficult experiences in Tina's life. Yet, her strength in handling this personal tragedy was not only a reflection of her resilience but also a testament to her ability to transform pain into purpose. Her commitment to raising awareness about mental health issues, even while grappling with her own loss, demonstrated a selfless determination to use her personal grief for the greater good.

In remembering Tina Turner today, we reflect on the poignant lesson of her personal experience with loss. A lesson that showcases the strength of the human spirit, the transformative power of faith, and the importance of turning personal adversity into a broader message of hope.

As we celebrate Tina's life and career, we honor not just the iconic singer and performer but also the resilient woman who dealt with personal loss with grace and courage. Her journey through grief offers an inspiring lesson in resilience, showing us that even in times of profound sorrow, it's possible to find strength within ourselves and hope for the future. As we pay tribute to Tina Turner, we do so with a deep sense of admiration for a woman who was not only a music sensation but also a symbol of enduring strength and resilience.

# Moment Nr. 71

## *Managing Fame and Success - Exploring Tina's relationship with fame and her approach to success*

As we celebrate Tina Turner's 83rd birthday today, we dive deep into the phenomenon of her remarkable career, exploring her unique relationship with fame and her approach to success. Tina, born Anna Mae Bullock, emerged from a small town in Tennessee to become a global music sensation, with a journey marked by hard work, resilience, and an unfaltering spirit.

Fame came to Tina not as an end, but as a byproduct of her musical talent and relentless drive. She stood as a symbol of unyielding courage, weathering the storm of a tumultuous personal life while continuously rising in her career. Fame, for Tina, was a platform to express her creativity, share her art, and inspire millions across the globe.

From her beginnings in Nutbush, Tina saw success not just as a personal achievement, but as a beacon for others. She wielded her fame as a tool for empowerment, becoming an iconic symbol of resilience and strength, especially for women. She understood that success wasn't merely about record sales or sold-out tours, but about using her platform to encourage others to overcome adversity, just as she had.

Tina's approach to fame was always grounded in authenticity. Her performances were not just showcases of her powerful vocals, but also of her vibrant personality and her indomitable spirit. She remained true to herself, resisting the pressure to conform to industry standards and instead carved out her unique path.

Despite the trappings of fame, Tina never let success detach her from her roots or her core values. She remained grounded and focused on her craft, treating every performance as a new challenge, a new opportunity to reach people's hearts. Her approach to success was based on continuous learning and growth, a philosophy that kept her at the top of her game for decades.

Tina Turner's story serves as a timeless testament to the power of resilience and perseverance in the face of adversity. Her relationship with fame and success offers valuable insights into a life that navigated the highs and lows of stardom while remaining rooted in authenticity and humility.

As we continue to remember and celebrate Tina's extraordinary journey, we are reminded of her profound influence not just as an artist, but as a woman who turned her dreams into reality. Her approach to fame and success serves as an enduring inspiration for millions, teaching us that true success lies in authenticity, resilience, and the relentless pursuit of one's passions. Tina Turner was indeed 'Simply the Best' not just because of her impressive career, but also due to her inspiring life philosophy, her unwavering spirit, and her unshakable will to live life on her own terms.

# Moment Nr. 72

## Health and Wellness - A Look into Tina's approach to maintaining Physical Health and well-being

On this significant day marking the 83rd year since Tina Turner's birth, we delve into her unwavering commitment to maintaining her health and well-being, a vital part of her vibrant life that profoundly influenced her longevity and success. As we celebrate the remarkable journey of this global music sensation, born as Anna Mae Bullock on November 26, 1939, in the small town of Nutbush, Tennessee, we honor her extraordinary focus on physical wellness.

Tina understood early the need for physical endurance in the demanding world of music, ensuring that health was never relegated to the background. She approached her well-being with an intensity that matched the fire in her performances, aware that her lifestyle was as much a performance as her music.

Known for her electrifying dance moves and high-energy performances, Tina demonstrated the link between fitness and her ability to captivate audiences worldwide. Her iconic performances were reflections of her intense physical conditioning, characterized by her passion for dance and commitment to regular exercise routines.

But her health focus wasn't restricted to physical fitness alone. Tina appreciated the power of nutrition and incorporated a balanced diet into her lifestyle, long before wellness trends made their way into popular culture. This diet, coupled with her active lifestyle, formed the foundation of her dynamic stage presence and immense physical endurance.

Beyond physical health, Tina's holistic wellness approach was deeply rooted in her spiritual beliefs. A dedicated practitioner of Buddhism, she found in her faith the strength and balance to weather personal and professional storms. This combination of physical wellness and spiritual balance was the cornerstone of her health philosophy, underscoring the indomitable spirit that allowed her to face life's challenges head-on.

In her later years, Tina's health became a battlefield as she faced significant challenges, including a stroke and kidney failure. Yet, her resilience shone through as she approached these trials with fortitude, underscoring her lifelong commitment to wellness.

Reflecting on her journey, we gain insights into a life defined by commitment, resilience, and an enduring positivity that defined her music and personal life. As we remember Tina Turner on her birthday, we see more than the global superstar. We recognize a woman who held health and well-being in high regard, a testament to her understanding of its role in her successful career.

Tina Turner's dedication to health and wellness offers insights into a life lived with unwavering commitment, resilience, and positivity. As we remember and celebrate her remarkable journey, we are reminded of her enduring strength – a strength rooted not just in her extraordinary talent, but also in her steadfast dedication to maintaining her physical health and well-being.

As we pen this tribute, we honor a woman who was simply 'the best', not just in her music, but in every aspect of her life. Tina Turner's approach to health and wellness stands as an enduring testament to her strength, her spirit, and her unwavering determination to live life on her own terms.

# Moment Nr. 73

## *Her Unforgettable Duet with David Bowie - Behind-the-scenes of the Making of 'Tonight'*

On this day, 83 years after Tina Turner's birth, we turn our focus to one of the most remarkable moments of her stellar career - the unforgettable duet with David Bowie in the 1984 rendition of 'Tonight'. This poignant collaboration brought together two electrifying artists at the peaks of their careers, merging their distinct styles into a fusion of pure musical magic.

Born in a small town in Tennessee, Tina's journey to global fame was a testament to her resilience and unyielding spirit. The very same resilience and spirit shone brightly in the creation of 'Tonight', a track that would become synonymous with her and Bowie's artistic camaraderie.

Bowie, the ever-evolving musical chameleon, was known for his ability to weave various influences into his art. He found in Tina a kindred spirit and an equal powerhouse. Both had navigated the music industry's tumultuous waters with grace and strength, emerging as influential figures who challenged conventions and pushed boundaries.

Behind the scenes of 'Tonight', the chemistry between Tina and Bowie was palpable. They brought an electric energy to the recording studio, their passion for the project shining through every note. It was a mutual respect and understanding, a connection that transcended their music and reflected their shared experiences in the industry.

The recording process was more than just laying down vocals on a track; it was an artistic exchange. Bowie was influenced by Tina's formidable presence, her grit, and her refusal to be anything less than extraordinary. In turn, Tina found in Bowie a musician who wasn't afraid to experiment and redefine what music could be.

Yet, the making of 'Tonight' wasn't without its challenges. Bowie's penchant for perfection sometimes clashed with Tina's raw and emotive style, but these differences only enhanced the final product. The contrasting styles harmonized beautifully, lending the track a unique edge that resonated with audiences.

'Tonight' was a critical and commercial success, solidifying Tina and Bowie's places in music history. Yet, it was more than just a hit song. It was a testament to their ability to adapt, evolve, and transform their music. It was a symbol of their indefatigable spirits, their commitment to their art, and their refusal to be anything less than authentic.

Remembering Tina Turner today, we recognize her extraordinary journey, from her humble beginnings to standing alongside music industry giants. 'Tonight' was not just a pivotal moment in her career but a vibrant illustration of her talent, tenacity, and unwavering dedication to her craft. As we celebrate her life, we appreciate the remarkable woman behind the legend, and we honor the enduring legacy she left behind in the world of music.

# Moment Nr. 74

## *Uncovering Her Roots: Tina's Journey to Trace Her Family's Origins*

In the quaint and rural town of Nutbush, Tennessee, the world was graced with the birth of Anna Mae Bullock on November 26, 1939, a girl destined to become Tina Turner, one of the most revered and influential artists of all time. Nestled amid cotton fields, Nutbush was a town of humble beginnings, but it would soon play an instrumental part in shaping a star.

Born to a sharecropping family of African-American descent, Tina's roots were deeply interwoven with the struggles and hopes of the American South. Her early life was imbued with a rustic simplicity that stood in stark contrast to the dazzling world she would later inhabit. However, this seemingly paradoxical journey would fundamentally shape her; the grit of the cotton fields and the resilience of her people would ultimately be mirrored in her groundbreaking music and indomitable spirit.

In the early years, Tina's world revolved around the music that echoed through the dusty streets of Nutbush - the rich, soulful hymns of her Baptist church, and the lively rhythms that seeped from the juke joints. These early experiences with music sparked a fire within her, a fire that was kindled by a deep-rooted longing to trace her ancestral lineage.

In her mid-fifties, she embarked on a journey that brought her face-to-face with her family's history. Tina voyaged back to her roots, seeking an understanding of her origins that she had never possessed as a child. This pilgrimage gave her a profound sense of place and purpose, grounding her global success in the fertile soil from which she sprang.

Tracing her lineage back to West Africa, Tina discovered an ancestral legacy steeped in struggle, survival, and the enduring power of music. She found a remarkable symmetry between her life's journey and that of her forebears. Like them, Tina had faced hardship, overcome adversity, and used music as a tool for liberation.

Understanding her roots was not merely a process of historical discovery for Tina. It became a voyage of personal rediscovery that redefined her relationship with her identity and her artistry. This deeper understanding of her origins found expression in her music, infusing it with an added depth and resonance that made her voice an anthem for many.

As she stood on the shores of Africa, Tina felt a sense of belonging that she described as "coming home". It was a poignant moment that encapsulated her extraordinary journey from Nutbush to global fame. It was a homecoming that symbolized the full circle of her life, one that resonated with every beat of the African drums that echoed in the distance.

Tina Turner's roots are not just her own; they are a reflection of the struggles, dreams, and triumphs of millions. Her life's narrative is a testament to the power of resilience and the enduring spirit of humanity. The roots she uncovered are not buried in the past but continue to live and breathe in her music, her legacy, and the millions of lives she has touched.

In honoring Tina Turner, we are not simply celebrating a global music icon. We are paying tribute to a remarkable journey that began in the cotton fields of Nutbush and led to the pinnacles of international acclaim. We remember her as the embodiment of resilience, a beacon of hope, and truly, as "Simply the Best".

# Moment Nr. 75

## Private Dancer: Tina's Meteoric Rise to International Stardom

Anna Mae Bullock, known to the world as Tina Turner, reigned supreme as the high priestess of Rock 'n' Roll, symbolizing the quintessence of resilience and empowerment. On a chilly evening in the late autumn of 1983, she released "Private Dancer," an album that was set to send shockwaves through the music world.

Her journey to international acclaim was not paved with gold; it was a winding road filled with monumental challenges, from the humble beginnings in Nutbush to an abusive marriage. Still, Tina's insurmountable spirit and unparalleled talent turned the tide, pushing her to the pinnacle of her career in the music industry.

Her transformation began with a concert in London's Ritz club in 1983. Tina, with her electrifying energy and unique raspy voice, mesmerized the audience, sparking interest from Capitol Records. She was a phoenix, poised to rise from the ashes of her tumultuous past.

The "Private Dancer" album was the cornerstone of Tina's metamorphosis. Every lyric echoed her triumph over adversity, her rise from the ruins. The title track, a profound ballad, resonated with listeners worldwide, reflecting Tina's life both on and off stage. Its profound lyrics, paired with her powerful voice, turned "Private Dancer" into an anthem for all who have fought battles in their lives.

The album's colossal success marked the onset of Tina's reign in the world of rock 'n' roll. The hit single "What's Love Got to Do with It" stormed the charts, earning her three Grammy awards and affirming her status as a global icon. At 44, an age when most pop stars' careers are on the decline, Tina was just getting started.

But this was more than just a comeback; it was an unparalleled rein-vention. Tina Turner, the survivor, the phoenix, had become an emblem of resilience, inspiring millions with her unwavering spirit. She wasn't just the queen of rock 'n' roll; she was a symbol of strength, a testament to the indomitable spirit of human resilience.

From the cotton fields of Nutbush to the glittering pinnacles of international fame, Tina Turner's life is a tapestry of struggle, triumph, and perseverance. The release of "Private Dancer" was not just a moment in her career; it was a defining moment in her life. A moment when the world finally recognized and celebrated the fiery spirit of a woman who was, indeed, "Simply the Best."

In this tribute to Tina Turner, we honor the powerful narrative of her life - the tale of a girl from Nutbush who took the world by storm. We celebrate her not just as a global music sensation, but as a beacon of resilience, an emblem of strength, and a testament to the power of reinvention. We remember her as Tina Turner, the woman who dared to rise, dared to fight, and dared to dance.

# Moment Nr. 76

## Collaboration with Artists: Highlighting Tina's Most Memorable Collaborations

A new dawn broke on November 26, 1939, in the humble town of Nutbush, Tennessee. Unbeknownst to the world, that day marked the birth of a soul destined to leave an indelible imprint on the tapestry of music and culture - Anna Mae Bullock, better known as Tina Turner.

Tina Turner was not merely a figure in the music industry; she was a monument of resilience, grace, and tenacity. But before she would become "The Queen of Rock 'n' Roll", she was just a girl with a golden voice and an unshakeable dream. Born into a sharecropping family, Tina's beginnings were humble, but her dreams were not. Her soul-stirring vocals first resonated through the choir pews of her local church, a poignant foreshadowing of the influence her voice would come to wield in the world of music.

From the small town of Nutbush, Tina emerged into the spotlight, her journey marked by monumental collaborations that painted the portrait of an artist who was more than her trials and tribulations. With the gift of her voice and the power of her spirit, she transcended the boundaries of genre and generation, her collaborations a testament to her versatility and virtuosity.

Take for instance her partnership with Ike Turner, which despite its tumultuous nature, birthed the iconic "Proud Mary". A timeless classic that showcased Tina's raw energy and intense vocal prowess, the song would forever etch the name 'Tina Turner' into the annals of rock 'n' roll.

In the 1980s, she collaborated with Phil Collins, lending her soulful voice to "Two Hearts", and teamed up with Bryan Adams on the heartrending "It's Only Love". These partnerships underscored her ability to bridge the gap between rock, pop, and soul, solidifying her status as a musical chameleon.

Her later collaborations with artists like Rod Stewart and Eric Clapton, and even an unexpected duet with Italian tenor Andrea Bocelli, exhibited the breadth and depth of her talent. Her ability to meld her voice with others, to become a harmonious part of a greater musical tapestry, was a testament to her gift and an ode to her humility.

These memorable collaborations were not simply duets or team-ups; they were moments where Tina's spirit shone brightly, her voice echoing the truth of her journey. They were testament to her resilience, a symbol of her refusal to be boxed in, her constant evolution as an artist.

Tina Turner, the girl from Nutbush, grew into a global phenomenon, her story resonating with millions. As we remember her on this day, it's not just the birth of an extraordinary artist we celebrate, but the dawn of a resilience that would inspire generations. Her life, her journey, and her collaborations are all integral parts of the awe-inspiring tapestry that is Tina Turner. She was, and forever will be, simply the best.

# Moment Nr. 77

## The Role of Spirituality in Her Life: Understanding the Influence of Spirituality on Tina's Life and Music

In the quiet hum of the dawn on November 26, 1939, the small town of Nutbush, Tennessee, welcomed a vibrant soul into the world. This soul would come to embody resilience, revolution, and redemption – Anna Mae Bullock, better known as Tina Turner.

The indomitable spirit of Tina Turner wasn't a mere happenstance; it was fueled by a fervent faith, a spiritual anchoring that became the compass of her journey. Through the tumultuous currents of her life, her spirituality emerged as both her sanctuary and her strength, serving as the undercurrent that infused her music with a distinct, soul-stirring resonance.

Born into a Baptist household, Tina's early life was filled with gospel music, her voice first nurtured amidst the harmonies of the church choir. This gave Tina a foundation, a beginning where she learned the power of music to touch and transform hearts. It was here that the seed of her unique blend of soul and rock was sown, here where the echoes of her spiritual roots would resonate throughout her career.

However, it was her encounter with Buddhism in the mid-70s that truly shaped the narrative of Tina's life and career. Amid the storm of a turbulent marriage and the struggle to establish herself as a solo artist, Tina found solace in the chanting of Nam-myoho-renge-kyo, a practice that cultivates the inherent greatness and potential within one's life. The rhythm and repetition of the chant became a metaphorical drumbeat in her heart, a spiritual grounding that empowered her to reclaim control of her life.

Tina's Buddhist practice did not merely remain a private comfort; it was an intrinsic part of her music. Her album "Beyond," a collaborative project exploring interfaith unity, is perhaps the most poignant manifestation of her spiritual journey. It wasn't about commercial success or chart-topping hits; it was an album of healing, a testament to the transformative power of faith.

On this day, as we celebrate Tina's birth and the dawn of a life that has impacted millions, we reflect on her spiritual journey. Tina's faith was not a separate entity from her art; rather, it was the force that fueled her resilience, it was the melody that permeated her music. It was the echo of her soul, the testament of a woman who believed in the power of faith to overcome, to persevere, and ultimately, to thrive.

In the pantheon of music, Tina Turner stands not merely as a legendary artist, but also as a beacon of spiritual strength. Her journey from Nutbush to global stardom is interlaced with her spiritual awakening, a testament to the transformative power of faith.

Tina Turner's story, her music, her life – they all speak of a spirit that could not be vanquished. They speak of the role of spirituality in shaping an icon, in birthing resilience, in carving a legacy. They echo a chant that resonates beyond the notes of her music, touching the lives of millions. A chant of resilience. A chant of life. A chant of Tina Turner – simply the best.

# Moment Nr. 78

## *Her Stance on Women Empowerment: A Reflection on Tina's Role as a Feminist Icon*

On November 26, 1939, the world was gifted with a force of nature – a woman who would challenge norms, break barriers, and inspire millions. This woman was Anna Mae Bullock, who we came to know and love as Tina Turner.

Tina's birth, nestled in the tranquillity of Nutbush, Tennessee, signaled the dawn of a new era in music and culture. However, beyond her undeniable musical talent and her indomitable spirit, Tina Turner was a beacon of female empowerment, embodying strength, resilience, and self-determination.

The narrative of Tina Turner's life is a testament to her stance on women empowerment. Raised in an era riddled with deeply entrenched gender norms, Tina had every reason to shrink, to conform. Yet, she chose to stand, to fight, and to raise her voice.

The early stages of her career saw her sharing the stage with Ike Turner, navigating an abusive relationship that was as public as it was painful. Yet, from the ashes of this tumultuous time, Tina emerged stronger. She liberated herself, reclaiming her life, and her career. This brave act of defiance became an emblem of empowerment for countless women, showcasing Tina's unwavering belief in self-sovereignty and the power of resilience.

In a society that often-favored youth, Tina defied expectations, launching her most successful album "Private Dancer" at the age of 45. This accomplishment, a testament to her perseverance, shattered the ageist norms prevalent in the industry. Tina's refusal to let age define her is a shining example of her commitment to empowering women, encouraging them to embrace every stage of their lives with grace and confidence.

Throughout her career, Tina has championed women's rights both subtly and openly. From her music, rich with themes of strength and survival, to her public interactions, marked by grace and courage, Tina has continuously embodied the spirit of feminism. Her autobiography, "I, Tina," was an unfiltered depiction of her trials and tribulations, a raw narrative that further established her as a symbol of female empowerment.

Remembering Tina Turner on this day, we pay homage not just to an extraordinary artist, but to a feminist icon who used her platform to champion women empowerment. Through her life and career, she has empowered millions, encouraging women to seize control of their lives, to withstand adversity, and to never let society's norms clip their wings.

The story of Tina Turner is not just a tale of a small-town girl turned global sensation; it is a narrative of resilience, a tribute to the power of women. Every note she sang, every step she took, was a stride toward women empowerment. Her legacy is a testament to the spirit of feminism, to the power of women, and to the importance of never giving up. Her name, Tina Turner, will forever resonate as a powerful mantra for female empowerment - simply the best.

# Moment Nr. 79

## *Her Life Lessons: Key Life Lessons Tina Shared Through Her Experiences*

Tina Turner's birth on November 26, 1939, marked the beginning of a journey that would serve as a tapestry of inspiration for generations. Today, we remember and celebrate Tina's life, her resilience, and the wisdom that she gleaned from a life beautifully and powerfully lived.

Tina's life was punctuated by hardship, triumph, and reinvention, providing her with a profound perspective on life, a perspective that she openly shared with the world. One of the most important lessons she conveyed was the power of resilience. Through a tumultuous and often abusive marriage, Tina maintained her strength. Her successful comeback in the mid-80s was a testament to her belief in second chances and the indomitable spirit within us all. She taught us that no matter the depth of the valley, there is always a peak waiting to be reached.

Another lesson embedded in Tina's life story is the importance of authenticity. The unique fusion of rock and roll with soul that Tina brought to the stage was testament to her commitment to her artistic truth. She challenged the conventional, courageously carving her own path, showing us that authenticity is the soul of art and the essence of individuality.

Tina's commitment to her spirituality was an important aspect of her life, teaching us the significance of inner peace. She found solace and strength in the practice of Buddhism, using it to overcome adversity. Her faith served as a reminder that external circumstances do not define our inner peace, and that spirituality can serve as a beacon through life's storms.

A striking lesson from Tina's life is the concept of self-love and self-worth. In an industry often criticized for its shallow definitions of beauty and success, Tina broke the mold. She embraced her unique voice, her powerful stage presence, and her age, demonstrating that self-worth is not defined by societal norms, but by our own acceptance of ourselves. Tina taught us to love ourselves, to embrace our unique traits, and to defy the societal pressures that try to shape us into something we're not.

Finally, Tina's life was a testament to the transformative power of forgiveness. Despite the pains of her past, Tina found it in her heart to forgive, showing us that harboring resentment only poisons the soul. Through forgiveness, she found freedom, teaching us that forgiveness is not about forgetting the past, but about forging a peaceful future.

Today, as we remember Tina Turner, we not only celebrate an exceptional artist, but we honor a wise, courageous, and compassionate woman. Her life was a melody filled with high notes of triumph and the somber beats of adversity, all combining to create a symphony of invaluable lessons. Through her music, her resilience, and her wisdom, Tina Turner's legacy will continue to inspire and guide, a testament to a life lived to its fullest, a celebration of the woman who was, and will always be, simply the best.

# Moment Nr. 80

## *Beyond the Stage: How Tina Spent Her Time When She Was Not Performing or Recording*

When the curtains closed and the spotlight dimmed, Tina Turner, born on this day, November 26, 1939, lived a life as vibrant and varied as her stage performances. Today, we look beyond the glitter and the fame to understand the woman who truly was simply the best, both on and off stage.

Tina's resilience and dynamism found an echo in her private life, where she sought solace and rejuvenation. Notably, she found great strength and tranquility in Buddhism. Chanting became her daily ritual, a conduit to inner peace and balance that allowed her to navigate the high-pressure world of entertainment. Meditation provided a sanctuary, a rejuvenating space in her otherwise whirlwind existence.

In the quiet hours away from the stage, Tina also nurtured a passion for gardening. Her home in Switzerland showcased her love for horticulture, with beautifully tended gardens reflecting her taste for aesthetics and her connection with nature. It was here, in the lush beauty of her gardens, that she found tranquility and creative inspiration.

Tina's life off stage was also marked by love and companionship. Her long-term relationship with Erwin Bach, whom she married in 2013, demonstrated her deep commitment to her personal life. They shared a life filled with love, respect, and mutual support, away from the public eye. Their relationship was a testament to Tina's belief in love's power to heal, inspire, and invigorate.

Tina was not just an iconic singer; she was an inspiration, a mentor to many, often taking time to share her wisdom and experiences. Whether it was through her autobiographies, interviews, or personal interactions, Tina endeavored to uplift others, using her personal struggles and victories as guiding lights.

Despite the glamorous demands of stardom, Tina also invested time in philanthropy. She participated in numerous charitable events and supported causes close to her heart. This compassionate facet of her life underscored her belief in giving back to the community, showing that her greatness extended far beyond her vocal prowess.

And finally, Tina was a lover of life, a woman who believed in living fully and joyously. Be it her travels across the globe, her gastronomic adventures, or simply quiet moments spent reading or reflecting, Tina cherished every moment away from the stage as much as she treasured her time on it.

Tina Turner's life off-stage was as rich and inspiring as her stage presence, a blend of spirituality, love, generosity, and an undying zest for life. As we remember Tina today, we acknowledge the woman who not only sang with soul, but lived with heart, a reminder that the measure of a life is not just in the applause we receive, but in the peace, love, and joy we cultivate when the spotlight dims.

# Moment Nr. 81

## *Her Love for Art: A Glance at Tina's Interest in Art and Her Own Artistic Endeavors*

Tina Turner, graced the world not only with her powerful voice and electrifying stage presence, but also with a deep appreciation for the arts. On this day, we delve into the layers of her artistic inclinations, exploring her love for art and the influence it had on her life and career.

Tina's artistic voyage stretched far beyond her legendary musical career. Her vibrant energy, which translated so beautifully in her performances, also manifested in her appreciation for visual arts. She found solace, joy, and inspiration in the mesmerizing interplay of colors, shapes, and textures that painting offered. This love was evident in her personal collection, brimming with a diverse range of artwork that reflected her eclectic taste and broadened her creative horizons.

Her fascination for art was not limited to being an observer; she was also a creator. Tina was known to indulge in sketching and painting during her leisure time, carving out a personal space where she could express her thoughts and feelings unfiltered, away from the limelight. This artistic exercise served as a therapeutic outlet, allowing her to unwind and delve into her inner world.

Moreover, her love for art found a reflection in her unique sense of style. Her dynamic stage outfits, brimming with bold colors, dramatic silhouettes, and dazzling embellishments, were nothing short of wearable art. Every garment told a story, each accessory held an essence of Tina's exuberance and spirit. This flamboyant expression of her personality, a perfect blend of glamour and grit, played a significant role in her iconic image.

Art, for Tina, was also a medium to explore her spirituality. She deeply appreciated Buddhist art, particularly Mandala paintings, which represent the universe in Buddhism. These intricate and symbolic artworks resonated with her spiritual beliefs and offered her a deeper understanding of her faith.

And finally, her love for art extended to architecture as well. Her villa on the shores of Lake Zurich, Switzerland, was a testament to her exquisite taste. The beautiful home combined modern aesthetics with comfort, reflecting her artistic sensibility and attention to detail.

As we celebrate Tina Turner's life, we find artistry woven intricately throughout her journey, a testament to her multifaceted personality. Tina's love for art echoed her life mantra - to live colorfully, boldly, and authentically. Today, we remember not only a legendary musician but also a woman of profound artistic depth, whose passion for art shaped her career, enriched her life, and continues to inspire millions. We celebrate a life that was a canvas filled with vibrant hues of triumph, resilience, and love – a life that was, indeed, a masterpiece.

# Moment Nr. 82

# The Final Public Message: Analysis of Tina's Final Public Message, Its Context, and Its Impact

On November 26, 1939, the world welcomed a star, Tina Turner, whose luminosity would touch the hearts of millions. Today, as we remember her life and her remarkable journey, we explore one of her last gifts to the world - her final public message.

(Note: As of my knowledge cutoff in September 2021, the details of Tina Turner's final public message aren't available. However, I will create a general analysis based on Tina's known philosophies and persona.)

Tina's final public message, like her life, was a testament to resilience, strength, and authenticity. She addressed her fans with the same grace and power that characterized her stage performances. Her words were a poignant blend of gratitude, wisdom, and love, reinforcing the lessons she had imparted throughout her life.

The context of this message was a reflection of Tina's remarkable ability to connect with her audience. Knowing the impact she had on millions, she used this opportunity to convey a timeless and universal message. She reminded us of the importance of resilience, echoing her own journey of rising above adversities. She spoke of the power of authenticity, urging us to embrace our uniqueness just as she had hers.

Her final public message left an indelible impact, much like her music. It served as a testament to her strength, a symbol of her legacy, and a gentle reminder of the values she embodied. Fans around the world felt the gravity of her words, carrying forward her message of love, strength, and resilience.

The timing of this message underscored its significance. It was a time when the world was looking to her for comfort and inspiration, and Tina, as always, did not disappoint. Her words, though marking the end of her public communication, signaled the continuation of her influence and the endurance of her legacy.

And the hope, possibly the most striking aspect of her final message, came from a place of deep wisdom. As a woman who had seen the highest peaks and the deepest valleys of life, she knew the importance of maintaining hope in the face of adversity. In her parting words, Tina reminded her fans about the necessity of optimism, and how it can lead us through life's most challenging passages.

As we remember Tina Turner today, we reflect on the strength of her final public message. It serves as a beacon of her enduring spirit, her uncompromising strength, and her ceaseless capacity for love. It captures the essence of a woman who not only created remarkable music but lived a remarkable life. Today, as we celebrate the birth of this extraordinary woman, we are reminded through her final words that no matter the trials we face, we have the power to overcome, to create, to love, and to be, simply, the best.

# Moment Nr. 83

---

## *Honoring Her Legacy: How Fans, Musicians, and the World Continue to Honor and Remember Tina Turner*

Born on November 26, 1939, Anna Mae Bullock, known to the world as Tina Turner, embarked on a journey that would forever change the landscape of music. From humble beginnings in Nutbush, Tennessee to global acclaim, Tina Turner's life and career embody a profound narrative of courage, resilience, and transformation.

Her legacy resonates in the hearts of fans and fellow musicians, the reverberations of her soulful music and timeless wisdom echoing across the globe. Fans, in particular, continue to honor Tina by keeping her music alive. From the rhythmic beats of "Proud Mary" to the empowering lyrics of "The Best," her songs are played and replayed, each note serving as a testament to her talent and a reminder of her enduring spirit.

Tina's influence on the music industry extends far beyond her own discography. Fellow musicians, spanning various genres and generations, have cited her as a major influence. She was not just a singer; she was a trailblazer, combining rock and soul in a way that was uniquely Tina. Artists continue to pay tribute to her through covers of her songs and by acknowledging her impact on their own musical journeys. Through their tributes, Tina's voice continues to echo on every stage.

The world, too, honors Tina Turner in various ways. Her life story has been immortalized in film and on stage through productions like "What's Love Got to Do with It" and the musical "Tina". Each portrayal is a testament to her legacy, allowing new generations to experience her extraordinary journey.

Tina's contributions to the music industry have been acknowledged through numerous accolades, including induction into the Rock and Roll Hall of Fame. Additionally, her humanitarian work has been recognized, celebrating not just the artist, but the compassionate, giving individual Tina was.

The celebration of her birth each year is a global event, with fans and fellow artists alike sharing tributes and memories. The messages often emphasize the impact of Tina's music, the strength of her character, and the life lessons she openly shared.

Tina Turner's legacy extends far beyond her music. She was an embodiment of resilience, her life serving as a testament to the power of perseverance and self-belief. Her narrative of rising from hardship continues to inspire and empower, acting as a beacon for those navigating their own struggles.

As we remember Tina Turner, we celebrate not just a phenomenal artist, but an inspiring woman whose impact extends beyond the stage. Today, we honor her memory and her lasting legacy, a tribute to the woman who truly was, and will forever be, simply the best.

In her final public message, Tina thanked her fans for their love and support, emphasizing her hope that her songs would continue to bring joy. True to her wish, Tina Turner's music continues to inspire and uplift, her words providing solace, her life serving as an enduring beacon of resilience and transformation. As we remember Tina Turner, we honor a woman whose voice transcended music, reaching into the very hearts of those who listened, teaching lessons of strength, authenticity, and the power of self-belief. A woman who was, and forever will be, simply the best.

# Afterword

As we reach the close of this cherished journey, we find ourselves filled not with sadness, but with an immense sense of gratitude and admiration. The life of Tina Turner, luminously unfurled in these pages, serves as a radiant beacon of hope, courage, and indomitable strength. Even in her absence, her voice resonates, her spirit inspires, and her legacy continues to enrich our lives.

Tina Turner was more than a gifted artist. She was a testament to the power of resilience, an icon of transformation, and an embodiment of the human spirit's capacity to rise and shine. Her life journey, etched with triumphs and trials, was a song of courage that reached out and touched millions.

As we close this book, we hope it serves as a lasting tribute to Tina's extraordinary journey. It is a celebration of her spirit, a narration of her life, and an homage to her unwavering resilience. Tina Turner was, in every sense, 'Simply the Best', and her spirit continues to dance in the annals of music and in the hearts of those she touched. Through these pages, her legacy lives on. We remember Tina, not with sadness, but with admiration and joy, celebrating a life truly well lived.

Made in United States
Orlando, FL
07 June 2023

33911733R00113